More praise for
The Little Book of Courage

"A great resource for anyone who is dealing with the
challenges of life or a chronic health problem.
It reminds us that there is hope."

—ELIZABETH ROBBINS ESHELMAN, LCSW, co-author of
The Relaxation and *Stress Reduction Workbook*

"We all need to find our passages to courage. This book
is filled with such passages."

—ROBERT J. FUREY, Ph.D., author of *Called by Name*

"There is practical wisdom in this book. Don't just
read the wisdom, do it."

—DAVID REYNOLDS, Ph.D., author of
A Handbook for Constructive Living

"It's possible to read this book from beginning to end but, as
with a collection of short poems, it's more natural, and probably
more meaningful, simply to open it here or there—and absorb
what you have found. The genre is different, but the intent is
similar: to illuminate moments of crisis; to relate parables
of transformative action; and to provide vistas
of common human possibility."

—ROBERT HILL LONG, poet/author of
The Power to Die and *The Work of the Bow*

"Like a hot cup of tea on a cold, wintry night. *The Little B*
of Courage brings comfort and
and kind encouragement, the rea
own inner strength and compas

—JAMES BARAZ, meditatio
Spirit Rock Meditation Cen

"To fear is a lonely feeling indeed. In today's competitive society, to display any sign of weakness, much less fear, is considered abnormal. Yet all of us, big or small, have fears. *The Little Book of Courage* is one of those kind of books that a person can feel an affinity toward, like a friend. Reading it is like opening a country home recipe book filled with directions, ingredients, and anecdotes to relate to and feel safe, not intimidated. Unlike so many books, it is designed to keep, and to keep going back to for a re-read."

—VELMA WALLIS, author of *Alaska's Two Old Women*

The Little Book of Courage

The Little Book of Courage

A Three-Step Process to Overcome
Fear and Anxiety

Sarah Quigley and Dr. Marilyn Shroyer

CONARI PRESS
Berkeley, CA

Conari Press books are distributed by Publishers Group West

Cover and Book Design: Suzanne Albertson
Cover Photograph: © Tony Stone Images, Tony Cordoza

ISBN: 1-57324-811-8

This has been previously cataloged by the
Library of Congress under this title

Quigley, Pat.
Facing fear, finding courage : your path to peace of mind / Sarah
Quigley and Marily Shroyer.
p.   cm.
Includes bibliographical references and index.
ISBN 0-943233-72-0 (trade paper)
1. Fear. 2. Courage. 3. Peace of Mind.
I. Shroyer, Marilyn, 1944-   II. Title.
BF575.F2Q54   1996
152.4'6—dc20   95-49640 CIP

Printed in The United States of America
02 03 04 05   Data   10 9 8 7 6 5 4 3 2 1

Sarah's Dedication

To Matthew Quigley and Timothy Quigley, men of gentle strength, compassion, and courage.

Marilyn's Dedication

My admiration goes to my daughter Michelle, who has confronted her fears about major health problems all her life. Her courage and unfailing optimism have been a major source of inspiration for me.

My daughter Aimee has been faced with a loss of vision due to diabetes and has confronted that terror with a spiritual rebirth and inner vision for the future.

My sons, Rex and Reed, are a new generation of men who demonstrate courage through openness, compassion, and joyfulness. Their wives, Michelle and Audrey, present strength, hope, and creativity to the next generation they teach. I know my grandchildren, Erica, Olivia, and Tyler, will be involved in promoting profound change in a fearful world.

The Little Book of Courage

Transforming Fear   91

Contents

It's Okay to Be Afraid

Comforting formulas for getting rid of anxiety may be
just the wrong solution. Books about "peace of mind"
can be bad medicine. To be afraid when one
should be afraid is good sense.

—DOROTHY FOSDICK

Four years ago while I was having blood drawn, my arm started shaking. It wasn't the procedure itself that frightened me. With newly diagnosed neurological problems, I was frantic about what the test results might reveal.

"Are you scared?" the lab technician asked.

"Yes," I stammered, terribly embarrassed when I couldn't stop shaking.

"It's okay," she said softly. "It's okay."

I felt light years away from "okay." Being afraid while waiting to find out if I had a serious disease was perfectly natural, but I didn't know that. Driving home, I remember thinking I should have a bumper sticker that read: "The biggest coward in the universe is behind the wheel of this car."

Now I wish I could find the dear lab tech and thank her for her kindness. She could have lectured, "Shame on you—you're a grown woman," or, "Get a grip on yourself," but she didn't. Apparently, she already knew something I had to find out for myself: *It's okay to be afraid.*

Her words are a gentle summation of the beliefs that bind this little book together: It makes good sense to be afraid when your well-being or someone or something you love—your sweetheart or the planet—is threatened. It's instinctive to feel fear when the earth beneath you is rumbling, literally or figuratively. Fear tags along when you're anticipating new adventures or gathering up the courage to make changes in your life. There simply is no real reason to be ashamed of your fears, to apologize for having them, or to cover them up with bravado—"Who me? I'm not afraid!" *It's okay to be afraid.* In fact, acknowledging fear—facing it, feeling it—is the crucial first step toward transforming it.

This direct way of handling fear is not particularly popular right now. In general, our culture shames us for admitting to fear, expecting and applauding instant courage. When that doesn't work, we're encouraged to tranquilize fear with food, alcohol, drugs, television, casual sex, intellectualization, or shopping—with anything we can reach for to take the edge off its palpable presence.

Fear and those of us who admit to having it have gotten a bad rap lately. As Marilyn, a psychologist, and I were writing this book, we discovered a substantial body of current books, articles, and tapes that offer what sounds like a wonderful permanent solution to dealing with fear. These teachings deny its reality, asserting that fear is merely an imaginary something an individual's mind makes up as a product of a guilty ego. They advocate filling ourselves with love, which *is* real. Then, they promise, peace will take the place of all our fearful emotions. The idea that fear is an illusion we can completely and forever erase through various psychological and spiritual beliefs and practices is seductive. It would be a lot easier to be able to banish fear once and for all than to have to keep acknowledging it and deciding how to deal with it day after day.

We really would like to believe that fear can be dismissed like this, but we can't. During the three years it took to write *The Little Book of Courage,* we interviewed more than a hundred people, ages five through eighty-five, about their fears. Only one person, a woman, told us, "I'm not afraid of anything." All the rest let us in on their encounters with fear and told us some of the ways they go about finding courage. In addition, hundreds of writers, diverse in their spiritual and philosophical frameworks and spanning thousands of years, spoke to us about both fear and courage. In the reflections that follow, we draw from quite a few of our own experiences as well.

Though thoroughly convinced of the reality of fear and all too aware that we can't permanently escape from it, while Marilyn and I were writing, we couldn't resist wishing that life would grant us a sabbatical—just a short hiatus—from facing and feeling our own fears. It seemed only fair that the universe might free us from fear so we'd have more time and energy. Besides, both of us had already collected plenty of experiences—we didn't really need any new personal anecdotes for this book. Of course our wishful thinking got us nowhere. Brand-new material kept rolling in.

During this time, I faced neurological problems that left me with slight disabilities that may or may not get progressively worse. I'm having to learn to exist with ongoing fear and to go on, sans any illusion of certainty about the future. I doubt that peace of heart and mind will ever again be effortless or automatic and regard their visits as fresh miracles each time they arrive. Although it's not been easy, my situation continually reminds me that to handle my fears, I must face each one, allow it to arise, and, at times, further investigate it. The necessity of this sometimes very painful practice keeps opening my heart wider and wider to the topic of this book.

At the same time, Marilyn was going through a separation and divorce that activated old fears of abandonment and forced her to confront a complex court system and an intimidating lawyer. In addition, her two young adult daughters both became very ill several times, and one was in a serious automobile accident. Marilyn was afraid for them and was terrified, imagining the possibility of losing either one.

Writing many of these pages knee-deep in fear gave us opportunities to keep testing and refining the reflections that follow, and we can testify personally: *It's possible to experience real joy while facing and feeling our fears. By submitting to this simple process over and over, day after day, fear often changes into courage, kindness, compassion, wisdom, love, faith, patience, serenity, calm awareness, or acceptance. And even when a persistent fear won't budge, as we grow more accustomed to its presence, it can become more manageable.* To some degree, we knew all this before, but now, because of the latest chapters in our own lives, we know it much more deeply. We humbly offer these pages to each one of you, trusting you'll find encouragement no matter what you're facing—a final exam or the final few months of your life.

The Exit Ramp to Eden Is Closed

If we stop and reflect on what we're afraid of, often we'll find we're carrying around a bag that contains a couple of very heavy, horrendous fears, plus an assortment of more trivial but nonetheless worrisome ones. In this real world, as we look around us or survey our own hearts, we know that total freedom from fear is a lovely thought, not a likely reality.

Even if we believe in eternal life or reincarnation, every one of us must come to terms with the death of our present body; and before that, there are plenty of other things to scare us. Some of us are in awful physical pain, afraid we can't go on. Some of us have nightmares about getting sick, being hooked up to life-support machines, lingering long months before we die.

Others are afraid we're going to have to keep asking for a table-for-one forever. Or we're scared we'll never be able to climb out of a deep career rut but panicky about setting off into new territory. Perhaps we "have it all" and our fear centers around how we'd be able to go on if we lost even part of it. What if we suffered financial ruin and had to sleep on the street? What if someone we love died? Maybe we're afraid we won't always be able to dodge random violence or be someplace else when a natural disaster strikes. Some of us are out of step with society's values but we're afraid to go ahead and express our own. Perhaps we're older now, very lonely, and scared to death that we just can't summon our courage one more time to find ways to put any real meaning back into life.

Freedom from fear would mean we found our way back to Eden, to a garden where all living things grow and flourish in harmony, eternally alive—forever free from outer threats or inner struggles. But the exit ramp to Eden seems to be closed, permanently so far as anyone knows, at least in this incarnation.

Short of finding a way back to Eden, what we need for living in this real world is courage—*the quality of daring to crawl out from under the covers to respond to fear with fresh attention and appropriate responses.* The quotes, stories, ideas, suggestions, and experiences that follow explore many ways to go about cultivating this habit. The three separate sections— "Facing Fear," "Feeling Fear," and "Transforming Fear"— often overlap. Like life, they contain paradoxes and inconsistencies. Sometimes, one approach works—we need to greet our fear. Other times, the opposite is effective—it's time to tell fear, "Get lost!"

Though essays are arranged in a logical sequence, you may not need a whole primer of insights right now. Perhaps it's 2 A.M. and what you're searching for is one thought or suggestion to help you hold on until daylight. Maybe you have to give a speech tomorrow and you're shaking too much even to hold your notes and practice. Sometimes it's more helpful to read one pertinent quote and essay ten times than it is to read ten different ones. So feel free to skip around and find the one that calls to you right now.

All sixty-four essays are purposely short. Even if you're very frightened, it's not so overwhelming to spend just a few minutes reading, then to make even a small movement toward reconnecting with your courage. By the end of this book, we suspect you may become so accustomed to facing your fears that you'll need more good reading on the topic. Beginning on page 137, you'll find a list and brief descriptions of sources we found especially valuable.

Courage is a present from God or the universe to every single one of us. No matter how *uncourageous* you may feel, you're no exception—courage is inside you too. As consciousness of its presence grows, the reality of this amazing gift of grace is a huge relief: We have what we need—a seed of courage to begin facing and feeling our fears. As the habit of using our courage takes hold, we'll become more and more fearless. We'll be able to keep on crawling out from under the covers to face each and every fear.

Facing Fear

Not only Franklin Delano Roosevelt but also at least three luminaries before him—Montaigne, Bacon, and Thoreau—all made the same startling statement in only slightly different words. What they all said is that *the only thing we have to fear is fear itself.*

This makes a catchy sound bite, but it's no defense against fear. If we turn our backs on fear, we're at a disadvantage—we don't really know what we're up against until we face it and size it up. Fearing fear, in fact, can automatically freeze us in our tracks or cause us to run scared without even knowing what it is we're running from.

With help from our Higher Power—however we define it—from friends, from guides and teachers, and from the deepest part of ourselves, we can learn to manage fear by facing it head-on. *The only thing we really have to fear is fearing facing fear.*

Acknowledge the Reality of Fear

~

Acknowledging fear is not a cause for depression
or discouragement . . . The essence of cowardice is
not acknowledging the reality of fear.

—CHÖGYAM TRUNGPA

Are you ashamed of your fear? Do you believe you "shouldn't" feel afraid? Do you feel really guilty and inadequate that you just can't seem to shake it?

There is nothing we can do or think that will permanently erase the reality of fear, and hard scientific evidence supports this. Recent experiments with rodents show that the lowly amygdala, a dense nugget of nerve fibers near the base of the brain, senses fearful stimuli even when nerve connections to the cortex, the part of the brain where thoughts originate, have been severed. This leads scientists to believe that not just thoughts or beliefs activate fear, but that certain situations also stir this emotion *automatically* before we have any cognitive understanding of why. In *The Wall Street Journal* (September 29, 1993), Dr. Joseph LeDoux of New York University was quoted as saying, "We now believe that experiencing fear is an emotion that is 'hard-wired' into the brain."

Fear is a primitive, basic emotion that is built into us so we can survive. When we acknowledge it, we may feel cowardly, but we're not. For the essence of courage is admitting the reality of fear. We can take appropriate measures only after we notice fear's presence. Even when we misread fear or exaggerate it, there is no need to be depressed or discouraged. Instead, we can learn how to reevaluate a threat and get help if fear seems to flood everything.

Fear is a normal part of the daily kaleidoscope of emotions we experience in response to being fully alive. In fact, the more fully engaged we are, the longer our fear list may be. If you are a couch potato, you may be afraid only that a favorite TV show might be canceled; but if you are lobbying for environmental reform, you may fear the wrath of developers, corporations, and politicians.

What does acknowledging fear mean to you? Many of us have this equation: *I'm fearful therefore I'm weak*. As we learn not to be ashamed of our fear, we can change that to: *I'm afraid and I'm strong enough to face my fear.*

What do you suspect is activating the fear you're feeling? Exactly what is it that you're afraid of? A future event? A person? A touchy situation you see no way out of? A diagnosed or undiagnosed illness? A challenge at work? Relapsing into an addiction? Make your fears real and concrete by answering these questions as best you can. Like a stock clerk, take inventory of each fear without judging yourself. Just see each one and note it. Don't ignore fear, numb it, or intellectualize it away. It is a messenger, not a monster.

Find Fear's Message

~

Fear is an emotion indispensable for survival.

—HANNAH ARENDT

I love Arendt's quote because it points out the usefulness of fear. Not long ago, I heard a snippet of news on the radio about a schizophrenic man who was visiting a zoo. He wanted to pet the lions, so he jumped right into the lion's den. One of the lions swatted him, but he was lucky—he wound up in the emergency room needing only seventeen stitches.

Obviously, this man was *fearless,* but that wasn't such a good thing. Indeed, fearlessness such as his usually stems from an impairment in judgment. If we are mentally ill, drinking, or under the influence of drugs, or if we're inexperienced and naive, we may not even notice a potential danger; or, if we do, we may not be able to decide what to do about it.

Years ago in a lecture, psychiatrist-author M. Scott Peck put it bluntly: "The absence of fear is not courage, but some kind of brain damage." Being free from fear can be just plain stupid, foolish, or even fatal. Without fear to regulate our responses and actions, we may jaywalk across a superhighway, have intercourse without a condom with someone we barely know, or swim in waters marked *Danger—Strong undercurrents.*

I've been totally fearless only once—after swallowing two Valiums my doctor prescribed before a frightening medical procedure. The forty-five-minute ordeal didn't scare me at all, but if someone had yelled, "Fire! Fire!" I probably would have continued to lie there, just smiling, saying, "No problem. No problem." My too-tranquil state left me with no fight-or-flight response.

In *Moby Dick,* Herman Melville wrote, "The most reliable and useful courage is that which arises from the fair estimation of the encountered peril." Fear helps us do that. It's a messenger that delivers instructions: Proceed with caution. Run like mad. Stop. Or, Go on—try a new challenge; a little fear is natural and won't kill you.

We can learn to evaluate the information fear contains and put it to constructive use. Fear of relapsing into an addiction can lead us to attend support group meetings. Fear of a heart attack can motivate us to lower salt and fat intake, exercise, and relax. Fear of lingering for months hooked up to life-support machinery can make us sign a living will. Fear of never experiencing deep intimacy with our mate can lead us to put efforts into communicating and expressing our love in concrete ways. Fear of air pollution can motivate us to ride buses and form car pools.

To find the courage within you, give up the quest to become fearless. Concentrate instead on being *fear-conscious.* When you are afraid, ask yourself, What is my fear saying to me? What is the useful message in my feeling? Am I taking a realistic risk in quitting my job or buying this house, or am I putting myself too much in jeopardy?

This direct approach may seem scary at first—and you will no doubt make mistakes—but with practice, you'll gain more skill in interpreting fear. The biggest mistake is to keep ignoring or denying fear. Being open to receiving fear's messages is the best way to develop tough, reliable courage.

Respect All Your Fears

*No matter how irrational we may know any
particular fear to be, we need to treat our
fearful feelings with respect.*

—SHELDON KOPP

Sometimes seemingly silly things can really scare us. I'm not talking now about paralyzing phobias that require professional assistance. Here I'm taking a look at smaller, irrational fears, the ones that keep showing up as surely as flies at a picnic, not crippling us, but turning into pesky aggravations.

One such fear of mine is riding on a bus. It's not that I'm afraid of an accident; rather, I wonder if I'll recognize the right stop soon enough to reach up and yank the cord to signal the driver to stop. And once I manage that, I ask myself: Where do I catch the bus back? Over there, or over *there*?"

Social gatherings give me butterflies as well. I could never get a passing grade in Cocktail Banter 101. At parties, I feel like a hopeless klutz in a Ping-Pong match. Others keep hitting and returning the conversation ball. By the time I think of something to say, the ball's whizzed past and I've missed it.

If by this point you are wondering how in the world anyone who's been on this planet more than half a century could still be jittery about buses and parties, that's okay. My list of fears that don't make a lot of sense won't be the same as yours. What's on your list? Just taking them out of a plain brown wrapper and dumping them all on the table is the first step in overcoming shame about them and starting to respect them.

When we asked people to share their fears, we collected some that sounded pretty irrational: "getting hugged (no, not *mugged*—hugged!)," "roaches," "falling asleep without a light on," "the beginning and end of a vacation," "riding as a passenger in a car," and "appearing stupid." We tagged that last one "irrational" because the professor who admits to this fear is highly respected for her original research and inspired classroom lectures. Had she confessed a fear of not being on the best-dressed list, that would have made sense, but appearing stupid? That would enter no one else's mind but her own.

As you haul your fears out into the open, remember that all human beings, though they may not admit it, are afraid of things that hold little or no inherent danger. It helps too to remind yourself of all the things you don't fear or those things you have already come to terms with. I have, for instance, little fear of traveling alone on an airplane anyplace in the world; it's buses I can't take. (These are not supposed to make sense!) And when I wrote magazine articles, I overcame my fear of interviewing people, even famous ones. Once, I spent an entire relaxed day chatting with an Olympic gold medalist. But when I met him at a party months later....

There is comfort in knowing that often we have a choice to confront or to avoid our irrational fears. I choose to keep riding buses, and occasionally I go to parties. But no way will I snorkel in deep water or camp out in a small tent.

On your list, which ones do you want to confront? Which ones do you choose to run from? Your answers may change tomorrow. But respect yourself today for doing the deciding.

Know You Can Cope

~

At the bottom of every one of your fears is
simply the fear that you can't handle
whatever life may bring you.

—SUSAN JEFFERS, PH.D.

V alerie is not too sure that life begins at forty. As she enters her fourth decade, she's tired. During the past six years, a lot has happened. First, the business she and her husband worked hard to build went bankrupt. Then her teenage daughter was diagnosed with cancer and underwent chemotherapy. The daughter appears to be okay, but Valerie's husband just seriously injured his knee and was forced to stop working as a carpenter. He's now in training to learn computer programming. Meanwhile, Valerie, an office manager, was recently laid off. Money is tight, but she's decided to stay home for a few months to focus on her family and to rest up.

"I'm really scared about the next thing around the corner," Valerie says. "I don't know if I'm going to be able to deal with it or not. I'm just tired of handling everything that's come up. It seems like it's harder each time."

Valerie's afraid she's not made of the right stuff to keep trudging up hills that seem to be getting steeper and steeper. Her uncertainty is understandable. But when we lose our confidence like this, challenges are not just challenges anymore; they turn into stresses that can cause us to become totally exhausted, more vulnerable to illnesses, and burnt out.

According to psychologist Dr. Paul Pearsall, stress occurs when we perceive a threat to our physical or psychological well-being, *and* we perceive that our responses are inadequate to cope. There seems to be no way off the fear/stress-go-round unless we alter our interior monologues and dispel this fear-of-all-fears—the big, pervasive, underlying terror that we're simply not cut out to handle everything life throws at us.

But how can we see ourselves differently? At a University of Hawaii workshop called "The Illuminated Life," Professor Emeritus of Psychology Abe Arkoff offered the best answer I've ever heard. He says we need to take to heart and to keep remembering this one sentence: *Whatever happens, I will manage, I will manage.*

That sounds very nice, but I wondered if such unwavering self-confidence was actually possible, so I asked, "How can we be sure we'll manage all that well?"

Abe answered, "What terrorizes us is not that we won't manage well, but rather that we won't be able to manage *at all*—that an absolutely awful situation will occur. But even then, we have a choice. We can sink in defeat or we can tell ourselves: *I will manage, I will manage.* And we can ask ourselves, *What is the first step—one that I can take right now?* Sometimes we sink first, then after a while we get ourselves together, rise, and begin to manage. Ultimately, we *do* manage. We manage well or we manage badly, but knowing at the outset that we *can* manage, that we *will* manage, we are more likely to manage well."

Try on Abe's straightforward, liberating belief. Stop worrying about what grade you'll get on life's next test. Kindly and with great compassion, grant yourself permission to join the rest of struggling humankind. Just do the best you can. No one stays on the honor roll all the time. Maybe you'll ace some challenges and barely pass others. But you will manage. You *will* manage.

Put Your Fears on Paper

Whatever our crisis, whatever our sorrow, whatever
our feeling, to name it is to frame it. A frame of words
gives us the safety to claim our feelings as our own,
to become receptive to them, to express them.

—GABRIELE RICO

Four years ago, waiting to find out what unknown malady had made the left side of my body weak and uncoordinated, in between a CT scan, blood tests, and an MRI, I poured out in my journal desperate petitions like this one: "God help me. I am powerless over this fear and maybe this disease, whatever it is. Help me. Help me...."

In another entry, after finding out I'd suffered three small strokes, I finally named my most terrible fears: "I fear that I'll never feel really good again. Other fears nibble at me, but this one gnaws at me like a dog tearing away at a bone. I must measure my activities carefully. I tire easily. I scare easily. I feel as fragile as an eggshell. What to do with this fear? I used to think, *If you have your health, you have everything.* Now I struggle to put faith into new beliefs—I can learn to live, to be happy with less-than-glowing health. I can still go on as I am, not *was.*"

A spiral notebook and a pen. A computer keyboard waiting for our fingers. A box of crayons and a pad of paper. We already have the materials on hand to begin to tame our fears by framing them in our own unique words or pictures. Psychologists call this *externalization.* It is simply the process of taking something inside of ourselves and putting it outside in words or pictures so we can create some distance between us and our fears. Rather than feeling I *am* this fear, we can look at it on paper and say, "I *have* this fear."

What are you afraid of? Does it seem like such an absurd little fear that you're embarrassed even to admit it? Does it loom so large that you dread actually seeing its horrible reality revealed on a page? What is it that is stalking you? As the fear comes into your consciousness, don't let it take your breath away. Keep breathing in and out as you describe your fear in words or draw a picture of it. Then explore how the words or images make you feel. You may tap into sadness or rage. You may find humor or shame. Don't attempt to censor your responses or to dress up your state of mind. If it's unpresentable, so what? It's not going anywhere. It's between you and the paper.

One caution: If you get a sense that this exercise is far more hurtful than helpful, stop. Contact someone—a friend, family member, support group, or professional—to help you. But if you don't feel devastated as you write or draw, carry on.

It is common, in fact almost guaranteed, that you might feel sad or depressed initially. As you uncover uncomfortable feelings and look at tough situations, retreat may seem attractive. Just face what you can. Don't push too hard. Ultimately, you'll find getting it out of you brings at least *some* relief. Like strenuous physical exercise, this visceral-cerebral activity has cumulative, long-term benefits when you give it a regular slot in your life.

You can begin to form this habit today. Spend five or ten minutes putting on paper any irrational, desperate, or seemingly silly fears. Any at all. Your words or pictures will eventually help you evict your fears or coexist with them, bearing their presence with grace and dignity.

Understand That Worry Is Not Preparation

Worry is not preparation.

—CHERI HUBER

Many of us subscribe to magical thinking that says worrying prevents disaster. In therapy sessions, people often say to Marilyn, "I believe that worrying about something keeps it from happening." They view worry as insurance against bad fortune and do their best to control life by being conscientious worriers.

I too used to be a worrywart, but I've made a conscious effort to stop. Worrywarts believe that by worrying they are actually making preparations that will ward off frightening possibilities. For example, if I worry about my toddler falling down the basement steps, this will keep it from happening. Or so long as I'm worrying about dying, I won't die. But worry is only fooling us.

Imagining a worst-case scenario—your little one crumpled and bloodied, or you taking your last breath—is a healthy way to begin to face fear and decide what, if anything, you can do. Do you need a gate across the basement steps so your child won't fall? Is it time to acknowledge your mortality and focus on living until the moment you die?

But worry is not anything like this. When you worry, you allow your mind to explore every possible outcome, not once or twice, but over and over. You develop one scenario after another: maybe my child will fall while I'm answering the phone, or it could happen while I'm giving the baby a bath. Maybe I'll die all alone and no one will discover my body for days; maybe I'll be in a building when a bomb explodes. And on and on. Such extensive speculation is exhausting, and if or when you actually have to face the situation you've been worrying about, you may be too tired to deal with it.

My purpose in putting worry in this harsh light is not to say, "Shame on you for worrying." There's no need to worry about worrying! We all worry a little. A little worry as we meet harsh circumstances is natural. But worry turns into fear run amok if we keep inviting it into our minds, regarding it as a valuable tool.

The most effective way I've found to minimize worry is to see it for what it is—a false comfort and a dangerous substitute for preparation. To begin to give up worry, it helps to understand why you depend on it. Ask yourself: (1) Where did it come from, this idea that worry works magic? Were my parents expert worriers? Or were they so carefree that I decided *somebody* better worry? (2) What do I *really* get out of worrying? An upset stomach? High blood pressure? A feeling of self-righteousness? If self-inquiry doesn't help and you're suspecting that worry is worthless but you can't seem to give it up, talk with a therapist or a trusted friend who is not a worrywart.

To make preparations for any eventuality, look at what's worrying you. Imagine all that could happen—the best, the worst, everything you can think of—then *stop*. Now ask, What are my options? Is there anything I can do? Must I accept this situation and live with it? Must I live with the uncertainty of not yet knowing exactly what to do? Facing our fears directly like this—realistically surveying how we can best respond—is the hard work and the heart of real preparation.

Throw Out Hand-Me-Down Fears

⌒

Considering how many "be carefuls" our
parents bombarded us with, it is amazing we even
manage to walk out the front door!

—SUSAN JEFFERS, PH.D.

My husband, Jack, and I were about to go out the other day with our son Timothy and his fiancée, Rachael. Timothy was ready first, so I asked him, "Would you please make sure the stove's off while I put my shoes on?" He laughed, telling Rachael, "You see where I got my habit of having to check the stove every time we leave the house?"

When Timothy was growing up, unknowingly, but nevertheless consistently, I taught him certain fears. Another example I set: Be careful of other's rights, but be afraid to claim your own. It wasn't until he was older that I began to be assertive and to practice kindness toward myself. I was reminded of this recently when Timothy picked up new pants he'd left to be hemmed. In trying them on, he discovered they were much too short to wear rolled up, even though he'd clearly instructed the tailor on what he wanted. He was disappointed but almost took them this way. But then he spoke up, "This is not what I asked for." The sales clerk apologized, and within a couple of minutes a different, and this time very attentive, tailor was marking the hem on a new pair of pants.

Just as those pants weren't quite right, neither are our parents' fears the ones that we're necessarily comfortable wearing. As a young adult, Timothy is examining the "be carefuls" he grew up with and consciously deciding which to keep and which to discard. This sorting process is liberating at any age.

A simple way to begin is to ask yourself, What did my parents specifically tell me to be careful of? A second-generation Chinese American high school teacher in Honolulu remembers her parents repeatedly warning her about *haole* (a Hawaiian word used to denote Caucasian) men. "They are more like wild animals than refined Chinese," they told her, warning that marrying one would be a disaster. She disregarded their advice and is currently happily married to a *haole*.

Tanya, a lawyer in her late forties, says her mother taught her to be careful of *life* itself. For a long time, she was afraid of everything—of being herself, of taking risks. Once she became aware that her pervasive fear was rooted in her mother's timidity, she began to follow her own true desires. Recently, she went ahead and did what she'd been too scared to do before, closing up her posh suburban office, moving to the heart of the city, and reserving half her workday for those who can't afford to pay. Though her change was not accomplished without fear, it's *her* fear, not her mother's.

Almost all of us have suffered from adopting parental prejudices, prohibitions, and peculiar mind-sets. And almost all of us have been saved from harm by listening to our parents' wise "be carefuls." ("Look both ways before crossing the street." "Never get in a stranger's car.")

As we survey parental advice and look at the examples they set, we can keep the ones that reflect our values and come up with our own. No matter how deeply all these old "be carefuls" seemed to seep in, now it's our responsibility to carefully decide for ourselves exactly what we really need to be careful of.

Decide If This Is Fear or Phobia

Twenty million Americans have at least one phobia
severe enough to interfere with their daily functioning.

—NATIONAL INSTITUTE OF
MENTAL HEALTH

According to the *Encyclopedia of Psychology,* phobias are "fears which are persistently out of proportion to the real danger involved." Most psychologists believe that phobias result from *learned reactions* or *modeling.*

Here is an example of a learned reaction: When you were only two, your big sister repeatedly locked you in a closet; since then, you've felt uneasy in confined places. Claustrophobia doesn't overwhelm you until you're camping out in a tent and awaken frantic to get out. Here is an example of modeling: Your mother hated making decisions and manipulated others into making them for her. On rare occasions when she decided something on her own, she'd moan, "I've never made one good decision!" As an adult, you also hand others this responsibility and put yourself down about every decision you do make. You too have "decidophobia."

A phobia magnifies fear. A few bumps during a flight mean the plane is about to break apart. (The Boeing Corporation estimates that fifteen million Americans fear flying.) If you're agoraphobic, going out to a supermarket seems as hazardous as crossing the Sahara on foot.

Phobias most often show up in early adulthood; but at any age, the impact of a stressful or frightening event may turn realistic fears into a phobia. If you have AIDS, you may suddenly develop a horrible fear of doctors. If you were raped, stepping outside at night may provoke unspeakable terror. After a professor ridicules a speech, standing before a group may turn into a nightmare far worse than normal jitters.

Marilyn developed a math phobia in junior high during algebra class. In her late thirties, when she decided to pursue a Ph.D. in psychology, her biggest fear was that she might not pass statistics. As it turned out, after treatment for her phobia, she made an A. "My fear of numbers was finally cured after I saw that I really could learn how to use them," she says.

If a fear of yours has grown into a phobia, first define what it is that terrifies you: "I'm afraid to drive on bridges since the earthquake." Next, survey your options. Do you need an expert to help you shrink your fear back to normal size? If so, look for a therapist who specializes in anxiety disorders. Is it possible to live with the phobia without too much discomfort? Can you simply take another route and avoid bridges or whatever it is that's so scary? Or might you work up your courage enough to keep exposing yourself to your fear? After my strokes, I developed an intense fear of elevators but, denying my phobia even to myself, went ahead and leased a thirty-fifth-floor apartment. For months, I got on the elevator trembling, armed with a flashlight and a tranquilizer in my purse and a silent prayer in my heart. Being forced to ride up and down several times every day finally cured my phobia.

Whatever else you do, don't panic about your phobia. As Eugene Kennedy gently counsels, "We need not rid ourselves of troublesome behavior immediately. Whatever it is—phobias, obsessions, or depression—we can live with it for a while if we are intelligently and compassionately trying to understand it in terms of our overall personality."

Anchor Yourself in Today

⁓

There are years that ask questions
and years that answer.

—ZORA NEALE HURSTON

Is this period of your life punctuated with a question mark or even a whole page of them? Did you once think you knew exactly where you were headed, but now you don't have a clue? Do you fear the uncertainty and long for the security of the known?

We think we *must* know if and when we'll meet the man or woman with whom we'll live happily ever after. We think we *must* know if a cure for the disease that's afflicting us will come soon enough to save us. We think we *must* know if our training will lead to a career in our chosen field. We think we *must* know that our children will grow up to be happy, responsible adults. Yet sometimes, for weeks or years, life's big answers escape us.

My friend Jeanne, now in her midforties, is in one of those decidedly murky periods. She helps care for her brother who has AIDS and for her elderly father who has serious heart problems. An entrepreneur, she's now buying and restoring historic commercial buildings.

The two family members Jeanne spends most of her time with, and has grown so very attached to, could die at any time. The buildings she's refurbishing may not have a positive cash flow for who knows how long. Living with the fear of these uncertainties, Jeanne needed a reminder to celebrate each day rather than drown in the questions, so she designed a gold ring in the shape of a simple question mark.

Over coffee one day, she looked down at the week-old ring,

already scratched from daily wear, and said to me, "I don't even know all the questions anymore, much less the answers."

Though despair visits her often enough, this time Jeanne laughs. Her laughter is hearty and humble. It's one way those of us who are recovering know-it-alls express our relief at finding out that not knowing does not have to annihilate us and that certainty is an illusion anyway.

Unfortunately, these insights slip out of our fingers as easily as a wet bar of soap. Even once we know that we must live without all the answers, our mind has a way of making us keep wishing we could and then when we can't, of concocting a thousand fears about myriad uncertainties. When this happens, it helps to remind ourselves one more time: *Even though right now I can't know how anything's going to turn out, I can decide what I truly value, and I can live each day in accordance with those values.* With our focus on doing what we can right now, questions about next year lose their power to paralyze us with fear. And if we keep honoring the present, the answers that eventually unfold, though not in our control, will be outcomes we can live with.

Security lies in resisting insistent urges to know for sure what's ahead. Each time these urges enter your mind, acknowledge them, then refuse to give them any more attention. Instead, become conscious of your breathing and take a few moments just to feel the wonder of being alive in a human body. Then ask yourself, Are my actions and attitudes reflecting what I value? Gently redirect your energy and direction if necessary. Anchor yourself here, now. Celebrate each uncertain day.

Don't Be Afraid to Come as You Are

~

Being human means being less than perfect. Indeed,
perfectionism has been referred to as the fear of being
human. When you walk through the fear of being
human, you learn more and laugh more.

—ROBERT J. FUREY, PH.D.

We want to be perfect like a circle drawn with a compass,"
a gentle Buddhist teacher tells me. "But that's not necessarily perfection. The lopsided half-moon, that too is perfection."

True, but those of us who are inclined toward perfectionism would much prefer to be the neatly joined circle. A recent experience in my own life made me acutely aware of this. Last April, Marilyn and I had planned a week together for intensive work on this book. Just days before she was to leave Denver to fly to Honolulu to stay with me, I almost called her to cancel.

For a couple of months, I'd been in the midst of hellish and relentless menopause symptoms—insomnia, palpitations, anxiety, hot flashes, fatigue, trouble concentrating. How, I agonized, could I let even a dear friend see how far from perfectly I was negotiating this life passage? If Marilyn came, she'd see the dust and disorder in my home in paradise. She'd view firsthand the interviews, articles, and newspaper clippings that lay in random mounds covering most of the floor in my little office. She'd see I hadn't organized all the research we'd been gathering for a year and a half. But something stopped me from canceling. Probably, it was fatigue (it would take more energy to reschedule) mixed with vague hope that Nietchze was right when he observed, "Out of chaos comes a dancing star."

That week I felt shaky and out of kilter, but we had a lot of relaxed, productive work sessions. With our research in disarray, the essays we tackled grew out of our own deep knowledge about fear. After all, between the two of us, we'd had more than a hundred years to gather data! My too-pooped-to-be-perfect state that prevented my usual organization meant we had no choice but to express heartfelt ideas, to play with them, to bounce them off each other.

The night before Marilyn left, she and I sat eating take-out food and laughing, remembering the outlandish photo we'd had taken in grass skirts on Waikiki Beach. That same night, I sobbed in frustration, wondering out loud to her when or if I'd reclaim the stamina I once took for granted. And I questioned if I could, as Paul in the Bible did, find the courage to be content in whatever condition I was in. Her arm around my shoulder, her quiet consoling words let me know she accepted me as I was. And she helped me find the courage to begin doing that for myself.

We don't need to be neatly drawn, perfectly symmetrical circles. We are all a little bent and lopsided and full of fear. The fear of being human is one fear we can begin to lay to rest. When we do, we find we can encounter our other fears more easily, without the burden of perfection. We can also be with others without embellishing, concealing, or exaggerating who we are. There is joy when bare souls meet like this.

Find Supportive Listeners

~

*Being safe is about being seen and heard and allowed
to be who you are and to speak your truth.*

—RACHEL NAOMI REMEN, M.D.

Unlike many other people, I feel very safe when I visit my dentist. That's because the first time I sat down in Dr. Umeda's ominous mauve vinyl chair, I sensed a kindness in his brown eyes as he stared down at me and said, "Speak up if something hurts. Don't try to master the pain. Acknowledge it. Let me show you—do this if something hurts at all." He raised my left hand and moved it back and forth. "Just wave like that and I'll stop. Don't try to be brave." I sighed. It was a relief to know that I didn't even have to try to be courageous for him, that I could communicate honestly.

But often when we're afraid, it is a big deal to find a place where it's safe to speak about our fear. When people ask, "How are you?" usually they expect to hear "Fine, thank you," not, "I'm scared to death and don't know what to do next." It's not just strangers on elevators who are like this. Often it's brothers and sisters, mothers and fathers, spouses and lovers, even some friends. Sometimes it's because our expression of fear moves them to experience theirs, and they don't want to do that. So we pretend to be okay so they can avoid *their* fear.

It is gratifying to be able to say "I'm fine" and really mean it. But when we are hacking our way through a thick, tangled place where we can't see the forest for the trees, we need people who will listen then too. We need others who allow us to disclose to them exactly where we are, even when it's messy, confusing, scary, or embarrassing.

Many support groups provide a safe setting. Does a group already exist that deals with the situation you're facing? Ask around. Visit a group several times to find out for yourself if it's helpful. It's okay to leave if a group isn't right for you. After a few evenings, I stopped attending one twelve-step group that focused almost exclusively on blaming others and looking backward. I needed the company of others who, though struggling, were going forward.

If you can't find an existing group, how about starting your own? Nine months ago my friend David and I formed a group called "Facing Fear, Finding Courage." Anyone who wants to talk about the challenges he or she is facing is welcome. Five or six of us meet for two hours one evening a week. Our only rules are that we respect each individual's journey and keep everything confidential.

Keep believing in the necessity and the naturalness of your need to find a safe place to be seen and heard. Finding even one other person who will listen, hold our sharing in confidence, and treat us with respect lets us relax a little. Our fears are not unique. Others experience the same fears or variations of them. What is difficult sometimes is meeting others who are ready for company. There are many of us. Don't give up your search.

Be All Here, Now

~

It is not hard to live through a day if you can
live through a moment. What creates despair is the
imagination, which pretends there is a future and
insists on predicting millions of moments,
thousands of days, and so drains you that
you cannot live the moment at hand.

—ANDRE DUBUS

An ad in the *Honolulu Advertiser* lists the name and phone number of a well-known psychic. I keep thinking maybe I'd better call her. Surely some of my fears might shrink, or could at least be faced head-on, if she could tell me for sure what's going to happen next week, next year, or in the next century.

I doubt I'll ever call her, but I have often called on myself as if I possessed special gifts of forecasting. Recently, when I went in for a checkup, my neurologist noted a more pronounced shakiness and stiffness down the left side of my body. He called it something scary, prescribed medication, said it wasn't necessarily progressive, and encouraged me to keep exercising. I panicked. For four long months, I spent a lot of time predicting where all this might someday lead. I saw myself frozen, unable to move. I imagined my husband exhausted after years of caring for me, and myself heroically refusing to eat or drink so I could check out of my body when things got really, really bad. And then, exhausted, I conjured up a miracle—me running a ten-kilometer race in a totally healed body.

A little imagining of the worst and the possibility of miracles is okay, even healthy. We need to acknowledge terrible fears and to be open to wonderful solutions. But when we find our-selves heading off on regular, extended junkets into the future, the quality of life we have right now deteriorates. No one can be two places at once, even if one place is imaginary.

Eventually, I got tired of being absent to today. I realized that I could write ten thousand scripts in my mind and never convince the universe to buy even one. But as I discovered, it's difficult to accept that we cannot see into our own future. It's hard to admit we can't control the future by making predictions.

In a *Family Circus* cartoon, the little girl Dolly asks, "Will I ever see a tomorrow, Mommy? Each morning it's today again." If you're off fearing a tomorrow that never arrives, you can come back, but you'll need an anchor to help keep you here. For me, that anchor is a connection with my Higher Power.

So much of our fear is projections into the future. In part-nership with your spiritual source of power, let life unfold, scene by scene, starting right now. Morning, night, and often during the day, make this simple request: *Help me stay here, now.* When you need to, pour out prayers listing all your fears and asking for serenity to face them one at a time, if and when they should arrive. Spend a few quiet minutes just being aware of your breathing, silently saying "here" as you breathe in and "now" as you breathe out.

Stop trying to predict what's ahead. Accept the daily gift of grace to be fully here, right now. It is already yours so long as you keep asking for it.

Take Stock of What
You Can Count On

~~

Contact with facts brings equanimity, objectivity,
freshness, whereas flights into fancy land us
eventually in insecurity and apprehension.

—CARLOS G. VALLES

When we choose to take a risk or when life forces us to deal
with distressing events, often we imagine an array of
awful eventualities. For instance, once we put all our savings
into a down payment on a house and sign the papers, we might
begin to worry that a flood might come along and destroy our
dream home. Or we look at the quiet neighborhood we carefully picked and imagine a liquor store going up across the
street. Or we wonder if inspectors somehow missed the termites
in the walls.

If a mate has a heart attack and dies, we may agonize: What
if I'm too depressed ever to get out of bed again? How can I
handle working full time and take care of the kids all by
myself? Will I ever love anyone else again?

When visions of the worst possibilities begin gathering in
your mind, acknowledge them. If you can actually formulate a
plan to solve or prevent any of them, go ahead. If not, if you
must live with uncertainty or with the knowledge that resolu-
tion will have to unfold slowly, consider this very comforting
fact: Though there are no guarantees in this life, there are still
things we can count on in this moment—no matter what.

During the war in Vietnam, Buddhist monk Thich Nhat
Hanh lost all of his family, and the orphanage he and a group
of nuns founded was bombed and many of the children were

killed. He recalls that one thing that helped him to go on was to ask himself, What can I count on today? Some days it was only that the sun was shining or the rain was falling.

What facts can you count on today? Masahide wrote, "Since my house burned down, I now own a better view of the rising moon." All of us can find some real and actual things to depend on. Relax as you wait for answers. Be creative as you survey all your resources.

I have a friend who, in the midst of a painful divorce in which she was terrified of financial insecurity and being alone, used to ask herself upon awakening each morning, What three things can I count on today? When her mind began to wander into all the terrible tomorrows, she would gently bring it back to, Today I have a house and enough to eat and a job to go to.

It may be that we can count on someone we love. After Lydia put a down payment on a house, she began imagining herself losing her job and out on the street because she couldn't make the house payments. Frantic, she called her sister who assured her, "This is one fear you don't have to have. As long as I'm alive, you can stay with me. You'll never be homeless."

What can you count on today? A friend you can call any-time, night or day? A Higher Power to whom you can pray even when you have no words? A nurse who gives you a back rub every morning? A dog who goes wild, wagging her tail when you open the door? Your own dignity and integrity? No matter which of our fears materialize, we can always count on something.

Take Time Out

In the bigger scheme of things the universe is not asking us to do something, the universe is asking us to be
something. And that's a whole different thing.

—LUCILLE CLIFTON

For a decade, Marilyn specialized in sports psychology, working as a peak-performance coach for promising athletes. To help them reach the top, she showed them how to set measurable goals, take steps to reach them, and keep track of progress. She stressed that success depends on knowing what you want to accomplish and systematically pursuing clearly defined objectives.

For many years, every January 1, she followed her own advice, writing down goals for the coming year in perfectly measurable terms: earn $75,000 a year; see thirty clients each week; renovate rental property. Next, she'd map out strategies to reach each goal.

This New Year's Day was different. As she tried to focus on exactly what she wanted to accomplish, she couldn't come up with anything easy to measure. Instead, she saw single words in her mind—*integrity, courage, humility, patience, generosity, gratitude.*

Marilyn believed in these virtues before, but now something in her heart was telling her that she needed to put less emphasis on *doing* and more on *being*. "When you're used to proceeding straight toward concrete goals, this kind of nebulous call can stir anxiety," she says. "It's scary because there's no way to write out a blueprint or turn building character and gaining wisdom into a 'task.'"

When you begin to sense the universe asking you to focus on *being,* you too may be afraid of where you may wind up. You may feel as though the ground beneath you is opening up and wonder if you're about to fall into a deep crack, never to be heard from again. But this invitation is not about disappearing. It's about reconstructing your life, emphasizing *the inside out.* It's about emptying your mind of images of goodies and goals and simply sitting in silence, waiting to be instructed about what you can do that will truly reflect your values. It's about seeing what our fast-track culture refuses to acknowledge—that action verbs that propel us toward impressive destinations that signify status and success are not all there is in the rich language of life.

It takes courage to stop moving like an arrow straight toward tangible targets. When you slow down and take time out, some may think you've lost your edge, gotten lazy, or become ill. Fear of others' reactions could even make you stop before you start. Remember that "soul wellness" is more important than what anybody else thinks. Don't wait for a consensus.

Finally, don't turn this into one more stressful project. Take this simple instruction from Vietnamese Buddhist monk and peace activist Thich Nhat Hanh: "Don't just do something, sit there." Without a time frame, without any expectations of gaining anything, even something as noble as wisdom, just make time to quiet your mind. Eventually, regular reflection can help restore your soul. It can be a quiet space from which you clarify what your deepest intentions are and begin to see some ways to implement them. In other words, when you get up, you'll have a clearer vision of where you really want to go.

Beware of Catching Chronic Fear

I, a stranger and afraid/in a world I never made.

—A. E. HOUSMAN

The young man I met in the self-help section of a Houston bookstore was eager to tell somebody about his newfound freedom. "I can go anyplace now—into dangerous neighborhoods, even late at night, and I know I'll be protected," he said, "because I'm exuding peace and light." He went on and on, making an eloquent case for how an aura of invulnerability can shield all of us, if only we embrace it.

Though his view sounds comforting, not many of us can embrace it. Somebody we know has been raped, shot, mugged—or injured or murdered in a terrorist attack. As crime, violence, and acts of terror erupt randomly where we work and live, and all over, our fears hardly seem far-fetched. We wonder if we might be the next victim or if the awful thing that happened to us once might happen again.

It's easy in a frightening world like this to catch chronic fear—to become afraid of going out or staying in. To become too terrified to fly or to take a Greyhound bus. To be afraid, period. A robber or a madman could blow us away in an instant, but adrenaline shooting through our veins too much of the time could also shorten our lives. Our fight-or-flight alarm system can't always be activated without disrupting most of our bodily systems. Constant fear makes us more vulnerable to heart disease, high blood pressure, gastrointestinal disorders, and immune disorders.

We have plenty of reasons to be cautious, but we don't have to surrender to fright. We can make up our minds to find ways to minimize and manage our fear. Some people, fed up with drive-by shootings, stolen cars, and home break-ins, are leaving urban areas. Others wonder if the city where they live might be a prime spot for another terrorist attack, and moving to a small town or rural area is beginning to sound inviting. But those of us who can't relocate, or cannot imagine abandoning the metropolis we love, need to come up with specific tactics for making less-than-idyllic settings safer.

What exactly might you do? Buy a cellular phone and keep it charged and with you. Jog with a buddy and without earphones. Install floodlights and an alarm system. Get a dog with a big bark. Take a self-defense class. Join or organize a neighborhood watch group. Make friends with your neighbors.

Donate time, ideas, or money to local and national anti-crime efforts. Report crimes. But, as Greg MacAleese, founder of Crime Stoppers International, advises in a *USA Today* article, "Think twice before arming yourself." In his opinion, using a weapon in a dangerous situation "takes judgment and training. It's a tremendous responsibility." Be observant. If you overhear anyone bragging about plans to destroy a place or to hurt or kill others, take such assertions seriously. Discretely alert an appropriate agency—the FBI or local police.

To make a difference in a world you surely never would have made—to reclaim your community—become involved in finding solutions. Be careful. Be alert. And, knowing that you're doing everything you can think of to combat danger out there, be responsible for learning how to let go of the fear inside. Breathe deeply. Remind yourself that you can choose to relax and that you'll be much more prepared for real danger if chronic fear has not already worn you to a frazzle or made you sick.

Refuse to let awareness of danger stage a hostile takeover of your spirit and body. You have both a right to be afraid and a responsibility to handle your fear.

Form the Habit of Courage

How many small decisions accumulate to form a habit?

—SUSAN GRIFFIN

L earning to routinely face our fears may sound like an impossibly difficult task. And it's true that being at ease with confronting our fears directly takes tremendous courage. But that courage is available to all of us once we resolve to make small decisions that gradually undermine old fear-dodging habits. Each seemingly insignificant decision adds up. Little by little, one decision at a time, even if we feel like world-class cowards, we can face our fears.

Here are excerpts from the life of a lovely acquaintance of mine to illustrate how this can work: For many years, Ruth, now eighty-five, was a medical social worker. In 1963, she was flying back to Honolulu from Molokai, where she worked with leprosy patients, when the small Cessna in which she was a passenger crash-landed in the water. She suffered severe back injuries but somehow managed to climb out of the wreckage and swim to shore.

A month later when Ruth was discharged from the hospital, she went back to the beach to relax, only to find that being near the blue Pacific she'd loved since she was a little girl now terrified her. Nevertheless, she decided to keep returning to the same spot to sit and listen to the roar of the waves. Finally, one day she noticed her fears were gone, and once again the setting felt comforting.

Over the years, one decision at a time, Ruth continued refusing to let fear dominate her life. Today she bears the limitations of her old age with great dignity. She wears two hearing aids, has implants in both eyes, a knee replacement, and ongoing back pain. At times, she's a little uneasy about living alone in her apartment in a retirement high rise. To ease her fears, when she prepares a meal, she sets a timer in case she forgets to take a pan off a burner. She and a neighbor share one newspaper and made an agreement to put it in front of each other's door at a specified time every day. This way each knows the other is okay.

Ruth emphasizes that her faith is the source that gives her insight into how to meet each challenge. Ever since she was a young woman, prayer, meditation, and Bible reading have been a part of each day. Ruth believes that the habit of regularly staying in touch with the Divine Father is the primary reason she can honestly say, "I accept what comes my way. I don't hold a grudge. I don't think misfortune is necessarily a warning. I think it just 'is.' Things happen. That's life."

What small decisions can you make today to face your fears? Do you need to gently remind yourself to stop holding your breath, to relax, and to breathe in and out deeply? Is it time to start being firm with a relative who's dumping an unfair guilt load on you? Would it help to wake up thirty minutes earlier to meditate? Is it crucial to find a physician who'll communicate with you? Is this the day to go to an AA meeting? Are you ready to begin searching for the right spot for the restaurant you've been wanting to open?

What is life asking you to do today? Courageous people are simply creatures of habit. Right now you can begin to make small, manageable decisions that will accumulate to form the sturdy, heroic habit that is called courage.

Know We're All in This Together

~

Search the darkness, don't run from it./Night
travelers are full of light,/and you are, too;
don't leave this companionship.

—JELALUDDIN RUMI

As the great thirteenth-century Persian poet understood, we're all "night travelers" full of light, capable of giving each other companionship. A graduate student in her midtwenties grasped this too when she told me, "Once we realize that *everyone* fears something, we understand that we are not alone. If others can cope with fear, so can we."

As we go through each day facing our fears, in one sense we *do* walk alone. But it's immensely comforting to imagine and feel the spirit and energy, the companionship of others past, present, and future who come up against their own particular challenges. Our path *is* solitary, yet we're part of a vast, timeless, universal congregation making this journey.

At times when we're afraid, we may forget this, feeling utterly and desperately alone. We may convince ourselves that we are the only night traveler ever, surrounded by darkness, clutching one lone flickering candle. But if we look, we'll see others' lights all around—we were not singled out by the universe to face fear.

As our eyes adjust to the darkness, we'll see that every single one of us who confronts fear is a night traveler. Sometimes, our companion travelers have to go through hell, as children, women, and men dodging snipers' bullets in Sarajevo. As early Christians being led into the Coliseum to become food for lions. As millions of Jews tortured or murdered in World War II concentration camps. As African Americans in the 1960s refusing to sit in the back of the bus anymore. "As police officers and fire fighters, on September 11, 2001, braving danger, even losing their lives, in efforts to save others. As survivors whose loved ones left to board a flight or go to work that ordinary Tuesday morning and never returned home. As edgy dwellers in a world no longer neatly cordoned off into "safe" and "unsafe" places.

Night travelers must meet small terrors too. A five-year-old walks into kindergarten on the first day of school feeling lost and terrified. A young man rings the doorbell to meet his girlfriend's parents for the first time. An artist is a night traveler when she keeps making time to fill canvases with her visions. A heartbroken widower is a night traveler as he prepares a meal to eat by himself.

Lynn Andrews writes that "the first lesson of power is that we are alone. The last lesson of power is that we are all one." We must each find ways to summon our singular courage. Yet we can also dissolve into an oceanful of the fears, struggles, triumphs, and transformations of humankind, losing much of our lonely separateness. When we soften and become aware that so many others had to, have to, and will have to find and claim their courage too, we know we're all in this together.

In the closing lines of the poem that began this essay, Rumi added this beautiful promise: "The moon appears for night travelers." Once we crawl out of our solitary cells of fear into the companionship of other night travelers, we'll notice that it's no longer pitch black. When we light each other's way, the universe generously assists us, bathing our paths with moonlight, illuminating every dark fear so we can begin to face each one.

Treaʂure Temporarɣ Pleaʂureʂ

Everything you ever get is really just on loan.

—BARBARA KINGSOLVER

Years ago when I lived in Galveston, Texas, the mailbox half a block from my apartment blew away during Hurricane Jerry. Far worse damage occurred, but most of it was eventually repaired. I waited patiently for a new mailbox to appear, but it never did.

That blue receptacle was an important prop to me. I was working long hours completing a book. Many afternoons, just before the 2 P.M. pickup, I'd shut down the computer and stroll over there with letters or bills. Once out, why not get coffee at the Stop-N-Go beside the mailbox? Then, why not walk on over to the nearby Gulf, sit down, and let my legs hang over the sea wall? Twenty minutes out there with sea gulls squawking and dolphins dancing helped restore my soul. It makes no logical sense, but when the mailbox disappeared, the rest of that pleasant ritual died.

When things stay in place, we feel comfortable and secure. We know what we're going to do and who we're going to see. But sooner or later, big and little things that we'd let ourselves imagine were permanent disappear. A pet dies. Our best friend moves to a different state. A child grows up. A mate passes away. A support group stops meeting. One day we're baby boomers, the next we're eligible for senior discounts. And finally, even this body we were loaned has to be turned in.

The awareness that short- or long-term leases are all any of us can negotiate can make us permanently angry. How dare the great overseer of the universe take back any and every single thing! It's not fair. Or we can become obsessed with deep, ongoing fears that provoke agonizing speculation: I wonder if the stock market will crash. I wonder if the next big earthquake will swallow up me and my house.

To shrink our anger, to calm our fears, requires much of us. It helps to acknowledge that the single biggest challenge of human existence is coming to terms with this "on loan" life. Honor your anger and fear by facing them squarely. Don't try to run away from the facts, but don't allow them to spoil the ever-changing texture and content of each precious day. Mourn each painful loss and change. Celebrate losing the stuff you're just as happy to be rid of. Laugh about our common dilemma when you can. And play with what you've got right now.

Last week at Kailua Beach, I watched a little girl sculpting an elaborate sand castle. She was too absorbed even to notice me. The knowledge that her creation would soon be washed away didn't seem to matter. She was having a great time, and all her attention was on the moment. She's got the hang of it, and with practice, so can we.

Forgive Yourself for Being Human

Even Mother Teresa has heart disease.

—DEAN ORNISH

You're ill. Something has broken down. Something scary has entered your body, something you fear your negligence must surely have caused. You've had a heart attack or have cancer. You're HIV positive. Your back pain won't go away.

You're terrified it's somehow your fault. You've committed some grave human error. Perhaps you scoffed at vegetarian friends and kept on wolfing down burgers and fries. Maybe you reset the snooze alarm once too often and missed your morning jog or ditched Weight Watchers to hang out at the ice-cream parlor and devour hot-fudge sundaes. Perhaps you obsessed about the new guy who got your promotion, popping Maalox tablets to neutralize the bitter aftertaste of rage and disappointment. Or you learned to do visualizations but feel you didn't conjure up enough Technicolor images to zap your cancer cells. Maybe just once, or once too often, you didn't practice safe sex.

Sometimes, obviously, it *is* our fault. Ten years ago, Marvin was drinking heavily and accidentally shot himself. He says he looked down and saw a gun in his hand and a hole in his leg. Today, after four operations, the wound still oozes. He limps, and, at night especially, his leg aches. "That's the price I paid for being so damned dumb," he says, after eight years of sobriety.

Marvin has forgiven himself. And if you feel responsible for what's happened to you, you can too. But first, you have to resist sinking into permanent guilt. That option looks as comforting as a soft feather bed, but settling into a lengthy depression because you made an all-too-real, or even an imaginary, mistake won't help.

It is far from easy, but despite whatever you actually did or imagine you may have done, you can go on. The best way to stop obsessing about the past is to go back there one last time with the express purpose of hauling every vague guilt or acute regret out into the open.

How exactly do you think you contributed to your disability or illness? Stop right now and jot down, or recite to yourself, every big and little way you believe you messed up. Include even seemingly small infractions: I forgot to call my Mom on Mother's Day; I kept drinking gallons of coffee to stay awake on the graveyard shift. The accuracy of your perceptions doesn't matter so much as the acknowledgment of each perceived violation.

Once you've faced the fear that you're responsible and listed *everything* you can think of, acknowledge the anger and disgust, the sadness and regret, or anything else you feel. Then even if you don't yet feel like it, with the same compassion you would extend to a beloved friend, say to yourself: *I forgive you for being imperfect.* Each time you start to beat yourself up, stop and forgive yourself again and again and again.

Through all this, you've probably picked up insights into healthier living—wisdom you'd give anything to have had just a little sooner. Apply it now as best you can and lay to rest the need to know exactly what caused your condition. You can speculate and gather evidence forever, but there comes a point when you simply need to go on. Don't forget: Even saints and star athletes, no matter what they do, have bodies with limited warranties.

Feeling Fear

"Thanks to the human heart by which we live. Thanks to its tenderness, its joys, and fears." William Wordsworth's lines express gratitude for the wonder of our complex human hearts. Though we might wish they could always hold only deep reservoirs of love, joy, and peace, so long as we keep them open, they'll also feel gusts of bone-chilling fear, waves of turbulent anger, and stinging torrents of resentment.

We can't put up a security gate, allowing only joy and its close relatives entry while excluding fear and all its nasty kin. We have to feel fear too. It's not until we smell it, taste it, feel it that we can release it or at least see how best to manage it. There's no way to keep our hearts warm and tender without feeling *all* that stirs there.

Dare to Greet Your Fear

~

It is best not to say, "Go away, Fear. I don't like you.
You are not me." It is much more effective to say,
"Hello Fear. How are you today?"

—THICH NHAT HANH

Steve believed in a Higher Power, and for weeks he kept hearing that voice inside, urging him to spend time alone in a quiet place. Finally, one fall afternoon, he jumped into his jeep—his destination, a secluded lake. In his open vehicle, he looked up to see that thunderheads were building. "This is pretty stupid of me," he said aloud to himself, thinking he'd better turn around. But another voice was saying, Trust me, face your fear, go on.

At the lake, Steve climbed the ladder to the lifeguard tower and sat hugging his knees, looking out over the expanse of choppy blue-gray water. Then he started reflecting on an ongoing pattern in his life. In his thirty-six years, he'd gone from one romantic involvement to the next. In fact, not once since his late teens had he been without a girlfriend for more than a few weeks. The big bad fear he'd been running from all his life, the one he was attempting to face now, was an intense horror of being abandoned, of being permanently alone.

A few drops of rain began to fall, and Steve climbed down to leave. When it started to pour, he broke into a run, then stopped. He realized he was running from his fear as he'd always done. So he stood there, letting the big raindrops sting his face. Then, slowly, he walked to his jeep and drove home in the downpour. By the time he pulled into his driveway, he was drenched and shivering. But he realized: I didn't die in the rain, and I won't die if I'm alone either.

It may well take more than one dramatic encounter on a stormy afternoon to keep Steve's fear from ordering his actions. But by daring to confront it, it's no longer running amok in his mind. It has been faced and named. It's been eight weeks since that day, and he's deliberately delaying entering another relationship until he delves further into where the fear is coming from and what keeps feeding it.

How do we become brave enough to greet our fear as Steve did? Part of his courage came from his involvement in a support group for men and women addicted to relationships. But sometimes we gather courage all alone. We simply get tired of running from fear, and so we stop.

When we sense it's time to greet our fear, it's the act, not the flair or pizzazz we muster, that counts. We may greet fear nervously, stammering "H-h-h-hello, Fear." That's okay. Our lack of composure doesn't matter. If the confrontation causes us to shiver, we can wrap up in our grandmother's quilt or our favorite soft blanket. Or we can invite over a trusted buddy who will sit by us. We may do it dramatically, as Steve did, or we may not even leave our house. Maybe all you need to do is sit down and say, "Oh, hi, it's you again, Fear. Let's have a cup of tea. I need to know who you are and why you're hanging around." Then listen, remembering to be gentle and nonjudgmental as you open yourself to hearing. Each time you dare to make a direct inquiry into a fear that is ruling your life or simply spoiling your day, you are gathering vital information that will help liberate yourself from its domination.

Depend on Yourself

My life is absolute. No one can live it for me.
No one can feel it for me.

—CHARLOTTE JOKO BECK

There is much help, much solace we can find outside ourselves. Sometimes a friend's hug or phone call can fuel our courage. Often there is immense comfort in the company of a mate. There is insight to be gleaned from a good therapist or a wise spiritual teacher. But no one is going to provide us with all the answers or feel our feelings along with us.

When my son Timothy was four years old, the dentist used Novocain while filling a cavity of his. Afterward, Timothy was distressed about the numbness and wanted me to know exactly what this weird new experience was like. "Mommy, feel it," he begged, placing my hand on his jaw. "I can't feel it," I said. "I know it feels strange, but only *you* can feel it." He tried a couple more times, pressing my finger deeper into his skin, very disappointed that I could never actually feel it.

Even as adults, especially when we're anxious or afraid, we wish someone could feel our feelings so that finally we can move out of solitary confinement. And usually we don't stop at that. We spin a larger fantasy. Maybe that "someone" could also offer total understanding and, while they're at it, tell us what to do next, that is, provide us with the direction, courage, or resolve that alone we seem to lack.

And so we go looking, hoping to find a lover, spouse, friend, mother, father, therapist—someone—who finally will move into our experience so completely and intimately that we'll never again have to be alone with our fears. The problem is, no such person exists. And we don't like to believe that.

Indeed, it can make us madder than hell that there is no "feeling savior."

I'll never forget how my friend Nan expressed frustration about this reality. She'd been married thirty-five years, happily so, much of the time. But one day when she was feeling particularly misunderstood by her husband and not so sure she understood him either, she wailed, "No two people on this earth are compatible!"

Once we know that none of our human connections can offer total unity, that no two people can actually become one, we can begin to accept what Zen Buddhist master Robert Aitken calls "the biggest joke in the universe ... that there is nothing to depend upon." And when we see that? "Then we are free to get up when the alarm clock goes off."

It's an inescapable reality that it's up to us to crawl out from under the covers, rub the sleep from our eyes, and stay awake all day. And as soon as we stop looking for a savior, we can start to depend on ourselves to feel our own feelings and live our own lives. No one else anywhere is qualified for this unique job opportunity. Even so, especially at first, we may wonder if we're up to it and afraid that we're not. But with on-the-job training, our confidence will grow. There's a very deep satisfaction when we push past our fears and keep showing up for each day.

Listen to All Your Feelings

~

We are afraid to feel too much fear, hurt, sadness,
or anger, and oftentimes we are also afraid to
feel too much love, passion, or joy!

—SHAKTI GAWAIN

Not long ago, I heard psychologist Paul Pearsall speak about how we can heal ourselves emotionally, spiritually, and physically. Moved by music, slides, and his candid account of his suffering from and ultimate victory over bone cancer, three hundred of us in the audience found ourselves alternately crying and laughing over and over again.

An atmosphere where we're encouraged to be at ease with the flow of emotions is unusual. In our society, there is a widespread fear of experiencing feelings, coupled with fear of allowing them to be seen. We retreat into our heads, thinking about feelings instead of feeling them. We head into bars, sink into numbing depression, fill prescriptions for tranquilizers, sleep a lot or hardly at all, watch anything on TV, and say to ourselves and others, "I'm not afraid."

It's no wonder that feelings scare us. Early in life, our parents or other authority figures, afraid of their emotions, passed on their uneasiness to us. Shrieks of laughter, buckets of tears, fits of giggling—all the immoderate and spontaneous responses that give life texture—were sanded down into the smooth blandness of pleasant smiles or mild frowns.

Fortunately, it's possible to overcome early conditioning and begin to experience, and eventually even to welcome, all of our emotions. It may be that the fear you are currently struggling with, as you're forced to open your heart to it, will give you the confidence to let other feelings in too. Once you find that you can't wish away fear, ignore it, sleep it away, or eat it away, once you see that the only wise alternative left is to feel your fear, you can find the boldness to go ahead.

When you decide to dip your toe in the water to begin feeling the warm and cold currents of your emotions, you're making a courageous decision. But be prepared—you may feel very uncomfortable at first. You may feel painfully out of place when you cry at a loved one's funeral where everyone else is a granite boulder of composure. You may feel ridiculous when you laugh out loud about how great it is just being alive. The first few times you sit with your fears until you sense their retreat, you may feel skeptical, doubting it really happened. When warm compassion begins thawing your cool detachment, you may not know what to do.

In all honesty, it is likely that some degree of discomfort will continue. But gradually you'll learn to tolerate, then even welcome, all that stirs inside of you. For as you allow yourself to feel fear, hurt, sadness, and anger, you're also enlarging your capacity to feel joy, love, and passion. Feeling a full range of emotions is not only okay but also essential to life.

Feelings are like marching bands in a parade. Each follows a schedule that makes the parade—your life—flow. Don't order the melancholy band to play a more cheerful tune. Don't beg the happy band to stay a little longer. Don't try to cancel, detain, or hurry any band. Just let them all play. Your main responsibility is to take it all in—all of it.

Let Your Worst Fear Out of the Closet

~

To see and know the worst is to take from
Fear her main advantage.

—CHARLOTTE BRONTË

Sometimes the best thing to do with fear is to ask yourself, What is the worst thing that could happen? Then see how the story turns out. Usually, we're not too eager to try this. Remember the saying, *That which I feared most has come to pass?* Often our resistance is rooted in the belief that if we allow even a glimpse of the worst to flash through our mind, it might happen. Or we imagine that we could never be daring enough to look directly at a hideous fear.

The problem is, awareness of this most devastating of all outcomes is already floating in and out of our consciousness, making regular, ghostly appearances. And no matter how hard we try, we can't seem to stop its recurring theme: *Maybe the AIDS test will show that I'm HIV positive. Maybe I won't get custody of my son. Maybe I expanded the business too quickly, and I'll have to fire employees who are counting on me.*

The surfacing of awful possibilities like these is usually quickly followed by attempts to erase them. But they keep popping up again. So long as we keep running from our worst fear, it will tail us relentlessly, stirring up nebulous, debilitating anxiety. Only when we stop and shine a light into its face will we begin to manage it enough to start focusing on getting on with our lives—no matter what.

Five years ago, Marilyn had an opportunity to find out exactly how this works. "When my daughter Michelle told me her kidneys were failing, my life seemed surrounded by darkness. I was overtaken by an insurmountable fear that she was about to die, and I was helpless to do anything about it. But then the possibility emerged that I might be able to give her a kidney.

"There was no guarantee we'd be compatible and no promise that the kidney would even function. I could undergo the surgery, only to have my kidney rejected by her immune system. But actually facing that and verbalizing it to the hospital social worker helped me transform my worst fear from a horrible thought to a concrete possibility. I had to ask myself honestly if I could cope if my fear became reality, and I realized I could because my message to Michelle would still be loud and clear: *You are my precious child, and I will sacrifice what I can to make your life better.* Fortunately, her kidney transplant is still successful."

It may be time to pose the one question you've been avoiding: *What would I do if . . . happened?* Though the worst may be terrifying, brainstorm about how you might respond to it. Don't limit yourself. Let absurd, crazy, silly solutions arise right alongside wise-sounding, conventional ones. Now file these away and return to the present. Don't rush the process or demand an instant answer. In time, you *will* find viable options to help you feel adequately prepared for the worst. While it's not healthy to dwell obsessively on the worst possible scenario, neither is it wise to keep avoiding it. Once out in the open, the darkest fear has a shape and form we can grapple with.

"Do" Courage No Matter How You Feel

~

Feelings are for feeling.... They are to be noticed,
experienced, and accepted while we go about
doing what needs doing.

—DAVID K. REYNOLDS, PH.D.

In a Ziggy cartoon, Ziggy is all set to watch a TV newscast when the announcer says, "Sorry, folks, but I'm just not in a newsy mood tonight." One reason we're afraid to feel our feelings is that we fear they might take over like the announcer's did. As we know, it's easier to follow our feelings than to order them to follow us.

David Reynolds, an author, therapist, and the leading Western authority on Japanese psychotherapies, has developed ways of handling this challenge in teachings he calls Constructive Living. Its principles stress that to live satisfying lives, generally it works best for us to define our values and goals and to carry them out, no matter how we're feeling in a given moment.

In a New Dimensions Radio interview with Michael Toms, Reynolds explained: "In this culture we talk about feeling good about oneself or about controlling one's feelings, conquering one's fears. That's foolishness. Nobody does that. What you find, in the real world, is that people do courageous things scared to death."

Reynolds himself is scared to death to fly. He says he has a lot of insight about why he's afraid, but all that insight has never helped him alleviate the fear. Nevertheless, because one of his priorities is to lecture about Constructive Living all over the world, he gets on airplanes and estimates he's flown around the world twenty times.

Noticing our feelings while getting on with our lives is actually easier than repressing our emotions or letting our feelings dictate what to do. If we're depressed and do the dishes anyway, at least we're depressed in a clean kitchen. If we're terrified we won't be able to finish a big work project on time, breaking out of paralysis and putting in an hour or two more a day may not remove all our fears, but we'll nevertheless move toward completion.

Tonight I'm feeling a little tired and very unmotivated. Even though Marilyn and I believe wholeheartedly in the value of this book, even though writing it has been an enlightening, joyful experience, right now I'd rather be watching TV There's no need to repress my feelings. They're here in me. But I can note them and still stay right here, watching my blue computer screen fill up line by line with white words.

As I keep writing, I feel less tired, more motivated. Sometimes, as Reynolds points out, "Behavior wags the tail of feelings." That is, behavior can be used sensibly to produce an indirect influence on feelings.

To be aware of our feelings while acting is the essence of maturity. If we could do this 100 percent of the time, we'd probably levitate straight up off the planet. Meanwhile, as often as we can, we can keep feeling all our feelings while doing what we can and must. If your emotions are dictating your actions and keeping you from constructing the life you desire, you might want to read Reynold's book *Constructive Living* to find out more about how to "do" courage even when you're depressed, ill, or afraid.

Feeling Fear

Make Meditation Appointments

What makes life so frightening is that we let ourselves
be carried away by the garbage of our whirling minds.

—CHARLOTTE JOKO BECK

Practicing meditation—quieting our mind, observing, feeling, being with all that is happening in each moment—provides a structure for learning how to be comfortable feeling our fears. Meditation is about being awake sans activities or diversions. Initially, this makes most of us feel uneasy. Last year when Marilyn began meditating, often she'd get ready to begin, only to wind up phoning someone instead. We're used to doing something—working, volunteering, caring for our family, talking, making love, watching TV, eating, reading, exercising, driving, playing with our computer, petting the cat, or sleeping.

Our resistance is natural. But when our mind is manufacturing fears more quickly than we can face them, we may be desperate enough to push past our reservations. In other words, an ideal time to begin meditating is when we're most afraid.

Make regular meditation appointments with yourself. Every day, or at least four or five times a week, set aside ten minutes, gradually increasing to thirty minutes or an hour. Sit on a cushion on the floor in a comfortable position or in a chair, both feet touching the floor. Keep posture upright, shoulders relaxed. Cup your hands together loosely or rest them on your thighs. Gaze straight ahead, lips in a half smile. If you're bedridden, you can meditate lying down.

Begin by focusing on your breath. Breathe deeply, letting your belly rise with the in-breath. Feel breath coming in and going out, repeating to yourself, "In ... out." Keep using these words or pick others to coordinate with your breathing. Try "yes ... yes," "here ... now," or "let ... go" or allow other phrases to suggest themselves. As you use words to focus on your breathing, thoughts and feelings will show up, demanding, *Notice me too!* Go ahead. Acknowledge each one. Don't try to chase any thought or feeling away. Let each one come and then gently let it go.

Here's how a minute might unfold: "In ... out ... in ..." *I have so much to do. Did I remember to pay the phone bill?* Acknowledge the thoughts; simply call them thinking and go back to following your breath: "In ... out ..." *I'm afraid to tell Nancy I want to break our engagement. I'm a jerk.* Acknowledge the feelings. Go back to your breath: "In ... out ... in ... out ..." *My back aches. I'm sleepy. I'm terrified I'll hurt Nancy. But she's no saint either.* Acknowledge the feelings and thoughts. Don't resist them. Feel the feelings. Go back to following your breath.

Thoughts and feelings pass through our consciousness, but they're not really *us*. They're like clouds that appear in our mind. As we keep practicing meditation, we'll start to comprehend that we are more than even our wildest fearful thoughts or deepest feelings of terror and that none has the power to annihilate us. It's a huge relief to find out that we need only to *observe* them—that we don't have to believe every wispy thought or be carried away by every passing feeling. It's gratifying, in between their emergence, even if only for a few seconds, to experience a spacious, empty mind. But we can't capture that calmness either. Meditation slowly reveals to us how to accept each moment exactly as it is.

Befriend Your Orphaned Feelings

As we look into ourselves we see more clearly our
unexamined conflicts and fears, our frailties and
confusion. To witness this can be difficult.

—Jack Kornfield

Usually, we begin a meditation practice to quiet our fears
and increase our capacity to relax. Ongoing meditation
often shows us how to make these peaceful alterations. What
may come as a shock is that in the process of finding more
equanimity, we meet and must come to accept troubling aspects
of ourselves we never knew were there.

What happens is that as we spend time in meditation, our
thoughts and feelings—the ones that used to whiz past—now
begin to go by in slow motion. Instead of a disturbing blur of
garbage whirling in our minds, we start to see each little piece
clearly. Some recurring patterns of thoughts and feelings we
note are disgusting or terrifying. We see, for instance: *I pick a
fight with my husband every Sunday night and wake up angrier
than hell every Monday morning. I'm scared of practically
everything. I spend a lot of time trying to figure out how to
change people. I tell out-and-out lies when I'm afraid to say no,
and sometimes for no reason at all. I hate my mother.*

Instead of feeling great about having the courage to see all
this, we may become frightened and wonder if we should stop
meditating. Ongoing meditation is like turning on a flood-
light—there are times when letting so much light into our
awareness can be overwhelming. Sometimes, and this may happen after months or years of meditation, we need a therapist or
a meditation teacher with us, leading us more slowly, more gently into the light.

Our challenge as we continue meditating in the glare of our thoughts and feelings is to learn how to befriend ourselves, even as we're getting to know these rotten little details about our feelings. Our first response may be zealous resolutions—*I'll lick this! I'll fix that!* Or we may despair deciding—*There's too much to change. I give up.*

Meditation is not about doing or undoing anything in us. Meditation is about *noticing, noticing, noticing.* As we learn to notice all that's in us at a given moment, without analyzing or judging any of it, we can evolve naturally out of that awareness. The one thousandth time we're obsessing about our cancer recurring, we may finally say, *Enough. I'm tired of this.* Or maybe it will take ten thousand times.

By becoming friendly witnesses of everything in ourselves during meditation, slowly that mindfulness begins to spill into the rest of our lives. As we keep forming a more realistic, compassionate friendship with our own feelings, we begin to notice that it's easier to accept others. Gradually, as our mindfulness grows, we find courage to respond appropriately, heroically, and with originality to the person or situation at hand. Making fresh decisions moment by moment is both very difficult and very exciting. No two moments are ever the same, and the miracle of meditation is that by noticing the constantly changing feelings within ourselves, we begin to note *that* too.

Blow Panic Away with Your Breath

⁓

Panic is the paralyzing anticipatory fear
of being afraid.

—SHELDON KOPP

Don't panic! We say that to ourselves before the professor hands out questions for a final exam, while waiting a week for a biopsy report, when our fifteen-year-old daughter still hasn't opened the front door and it's three hours past her curfew, when we hear footsteps behind us in the dark. Anytime we're afraid that a situation might endanger us or someone else, especially someone we love or feel responsible for, our reaction is often panic.

When panic takes over, adrenaline flows and produces a state of heightened awareness that prepares us to stick around and face the danger or run as fast as we can. While we're trying to decide what to do, our heart may race. We may feel smothering sensations, dizziness, nausea, and chest pain. We may shake, tremble, or become frozen, paralyzed. All this overwhelms us so much that now we fear our fear and would do anything to escape it.

When you feel panic rushing through and over you, first and foremost, remember to breathe. Panic disrupts the most basic, crucial life-giving function of all: breathing. When you panic, you hold your breath or take only shallow breaths, so it's necessary to remind yourself to breathe in and out, deeply and slowly. Look down and make sure your abdomen is rising with each in-breath. Imagine yourself sinking into your breath, grounding yourself like a boulder firmly planted on solid ground.

Keep breathing, letting your muscles relax as much as you can. Even if you know nothing else for sure, know that you *can* keep on breathing. Comfort yourself with that reality. Gently say to yourself, *I'm alive. I'm still here. I'm breathing.*

Continue regular, deep, deliberate breathing, and as a sense of calm starts to take hold, evaluate your situation. If you are in a life-threatening circumstance, becoming calm will help you figure out what, if anything, you can do—run, scream, hide, or call 9-1-1.

If it's a less immediate threat, ask yourself, *Exactly what is it that I'm so afraid of? What specific fears might be generating panic?* If, for example, you're out of work and are sitting in a reception area waiting for an interview, are you afraid you can't buy groceries or pay the rent if you don't get this position? Are you dreading the interview itself? Do you already know you'd hate this kind of work, and now you're feeling trapped, wondering, *Why am I here?* Note each fear that comes into your consciousness—without judgment and without frantic attempts to erase it. Simply acknowledge, *I'm afraid of this, this, and this....*

Throughout this process, remember to keep breathing. When you're finished, take a deep breath and sigh. Now you know what it is that you fear. Though you may not yet know exactly what to do, you have begun to tame panic and restore your ability to think logically. Panic shrinks in the fresh air of conscious breathing and pales in the light of careful scrutiny.

Be Courageous Just for This Moment

~

The only courage that matters is the kind that
gets you from one minute to the next.

—MIGNON MCLAUGHLIN

At times, we're so scared that the idea of taking one day at a time seems about as possible as sprinting to the summit of Mt. Everest. It's more like, *Can I crawl through the next 60 seconds?* At these moments, we'd settle for even a modicum of courage.

Trust this reality: If you are alive, you can tap into your courage. Even when you're apparently out of courage, the truth is, you have some left. Take plenty of deep breaths, smile if you can, and try the following suggestions:

PRACTICE A FEW COURAGE RITUALS. A courage ritual is any regularly focused effort that helps you feel your fears and live with them when necessary, or to shoo them away when possible. The possibilities are endless. Here are a few: Practice gentle yoga stretches. Pray. Meditate. Read an inspirational book or listen to inspirational tapes. Listen to or make music. Work in your garden. Walk. Swim. Keep a journal, writing down exactly what you're afraid of. Do tai chi. Volunteer at a hospice, hospital, nursing home, animal shelter, or anyplace help is needed. Read the funnies. Find a "courage buddy," someone you trust and can talk with regularly. Take turns sharing fears, listening, and encouraging each other.

PROCRASTINATE. Why not put to positive use the natural inclination to postpone things? Remember Scarlet's motto in

Gone With the Wind: Sometimes we too need to say, "I'll think about that tomorrow." Say to yourself, *I'll wait to panic. I won't let fear take over until tomorrow.* For the rest of the day, immerse yourself in each moment. See your surroundings. Listen to sounds around you. Get busy or take a nap. Each time a fear intrudes, be blunt and firm. Tell it, *Not now, later.* This won't work forever, but it can give you a breather, a day or even a week off to clear your mind and help restore your perspective.

STOP LETTING YOUR FEAR TELL YOU THE SAME OLD STORY. Recurring fears come with a rut story that, in our minds, always ends in one inevitable, awful scene. For instance, anytime we have an argument with our husband, we conclude, *He'll leave me just like my first husband did.* To get out of a rut story, make up brand new endings: *He listens to me and I listen to him. We may not agree, but we respect each other's viewpoints. I tell him my fear and ask him to hold me.* Substituting entirely different endings gives us insights into how to make them come true. Even when a "happy" outcome truly is not possible, alternative endings help remind us that there *are* other ways, often more effective ones, to handle what we're afraid of.

BEFRIEND YOURSELF. Are you constantly telling yourself, *I'm a wimp. I shouldn't be so scared. Other people just go on, what's wrong with me?* It may seem phony at first, but you can stop mental put-downs and extend kind support to yourself as you would to a dear friend. Regularly and often, give yourself loving reassurance: *Of course I'm afraid. It's okay. I am getting through this. I'll make mistakes, but I trust myself to make the best decisions I can.*

Part with Pessimism

~

Pessimism is not inborn—we learn it from our parents,
our teachers, and our Little League coaches.

—MARTIN E. P. SELIGMAN

Karen, an executive in a large corporation, had a corner office with windows and the respect of her colleagues. But after a dozen years of upward mobility, she decided to resign. She wanted a flexible schedule and an arena in which to use her creativity more freely. Her plan was to put together her own consulting business.

The problem is, Karen is immobilized with fear. Day after day, she sits in front of her computer, trying to write a marketing brochure, but she can't get out even one sentence. She fears opening her business, imagining that when she calls on companies, doors will slam in her face. She keeps hearing the voice of her mother repeating, "You're so stupid." Then her father's voice chimes in: "You'll never make anything of yourself." Her fingers seem to prove their predictions—she can't even make them move.

Michelle, a single lawyer who just turned thirty, wants to get married but is afraid she never will. She's become pessimistic about the institution itself. "My mom and dad stayed married until my sister and I grew up. We had a stable life, but I have no idea how a man and woman who love each other treat each other. My mom always said, 'You don't want to get married.'"

Anthony frequently writes a letter, puts a stamp on it, then leaves it on his desk for a couple of weeks before mailing it. Friends look forward to hearing from him. He has a gift of telling the truth of his life in ways that make them feel less alone. But Anthony procrastinates because he's afraid no one can read his writing. He can't erase scenes from first grade, when his teacher kept holding up his papers, ridiculing his illegible writing in front of the whole class.

When we fear and expect the worst, our pessimism is like a weed in our life. Someone else may have planted it and watered it, but now it's up to us to spot it, remember how it got there if we can, and dig it up—pulling all of it out, including its deep, spreading roots.

What if clients actually make paper airplanes out of all our sales brochures? What if we say "I do" and end up with a broken heart? What if no one can read a single word of our scrawl? None of these outcomes would be fun, but none would be fatal. The pessimists who taught us the art of pessimism didn't understand the value of simply making an effort. They didn't encourage us to believe in our intrinsic value that is independent of any end result.

Fortunately, it's not too late to create your own reality. Pessimism is not a part *of* you—it was imparted *to* you. With new insight, with ongoing determination, you can discard erroneous negative beliefs and patterns of behavior.

Our fears are often markers that point the way to the changes we desire. If you're unable to go ahead with a simple act or a big decision, plant this new thought: *My true inner worth exists no matter what the outcome of my efforts.* You don't have to prove a thing.

Tell Fear Where to Go

[Fear] can never be overcome by fearing it. . . . you
fear it and it will grow in strength; swear at it,
send it to hell, whatever, but stand up to it.

—CATHERINE COOKSON

At times, fear can be like a solicitor who keeps ringing your doorbell, calling you at all hours, and following you around. Though you wish it would go away, though you try to ditch it, soon it becomes apparent—fear is not going to give up easily trying to convince you that you should be scared to death.

At times like this, fear becomes so intrusive and intimidating that you begin to think your only option is to keep running from it. But as the saying goes, you can run, but you can't hide. Even if we could run a four-minute mile or blast off into space, fear would be there waiting, smirking, "What took you so long?"

When fear takes over like this, the only way to weaken it to the point that it no longer dominates your life is to radically change your strategy. When fear seems as imposing as a sumo wrestler, what you must do is stop running, stand up to it, and make it totally clear that you refuse to allow it to remain a huge, terrifying presence in your life. You have to look at fear long enough to learn from it, then tell it to go straight to hell. You have to yell at it, snarl at it, show it your rage.

And don't forget to request extra help. If you believe in a Higher Power, converse regularly, relating exactly what's going on and asking the strong arms of the Almighty to help you subdue fear. Boldly request a guardian angel who's been pumping iron, a celestial bodyguard who'll stay right by your side.

It's fun to think about annihilating fear like this, to imagine reducing it to nothing more than a pile of ashes. It's also satisfying to remember past victories.

I'd already picked an incident to relate to you here—a time a year ago when I faced fear head-on and watched it fizzle out. But this was before I turned on the TV news this morning and watched a segment about a neurological disease that's a first cousin to the disorder I have. The guest being interviewed mentioned that her disease was in only its early stages. I've been feeling especially good for six months, but her words reminded me that no one, including my neurologist, has even a wild guess about how fast my impairments might progress or if they will get any worse at all. Thinking about this, I got angry all over again about being stuck with this disease and its nebulous prognosis. And I got really scared, hearing fear's voice: "Pretty slick, huh, giving you, a woman who used to think she could control her life, something like this. You *should* be afraid."

Just after this, I left my car at the gas station for an oil change. My hands shook when I tried to get the ignition key off the chain. The cashier kindly offered her help. Fear rode piggyback on my shoulders, weighing me down as I plodded back up the hill to my apartment. Inside, I kneeled beside my bed, asking my Higher Power to stand by me while I stood up to fear. I looked at all my fears and told them there was no way on this earth they were going to spoil the rest of the day—*no way*. This showdown was terrifying, but my fears backed off. They'll be back, of course; but one confrontation at a time, we can keep standing up to every single one of our fears.

Cultivate Calmness

~

Calm at first felt wrong because it felt strange.
I was used to the familiar—anxiety which
throbbed like fever.

—LUCY FREEMAN

Not long ago, at 6:30 A.M. in Honolulu, civil defense sirens began wailing. No hurricanes were brewing, so what was going on? Switching on the local TV news, I found out that because of an earthquake in Japan, the Hawaiian Islands were under a tsunami watch. All coastal areas were being evacuated; businesses and schools never even opened. For six hours everyone waited, wondering if a tidal wave would sweep over coastal areas, breaking apart everything in its path.

My high-rise apartment is at a safe elevation. I was in no personal danger, and it was very unlikely, given advanced warning, that anyone would be hurt. But I started getting scared anyway. Listening to news reports, seeing TV camera shots of Waikiki Beach without a soul there, looking down on almost empty highways and streets below—the atmosphere was charged with anxiety.

Some of us grew up in homes where it may have seemed as though we were constantly under a tsunami watch. Maybe our mom tried to wish courage out of bottles of booze, or our sad, nervous father always had a cigarette dangling from his fingers. Or perhaps our parents were drama junkies, generating crisis after crisis to feel more alive.

Some of us had parents who did a good job of modeling calmness. It was life itself, or what happened to us along the way, that put us on edge. Women who've been raped often report suddenly becoming afraid of such normal activities as going to the supermarket. They may have been calm before, but their calmness has been stolen. Veterans of wars and survivors of accidents or natural catastrophes may suddenly be susceptible to exaggerated fears and anxiety, as may those who live with life-threatening illnesses or disabilities.

Even if our families or life events predispose us to fear, we can learn to be calm. One of the biggest obstacles when we begin trying is that calm just doesn't feel normal. We're not used to it. We wonder what we'll be left with if we don't have anxiety throbbing like a fever. We may fear that being calm will make us feel dull, even dead.

Bewildered, you may decide it isn't worth the effort. But don't give up too soon! Get help from a therapist if you need it. Anxiety is addictive and hard to relinquish, but it's crucial that calm win out. Ongoing anxiety clouds logic, destroys joy and serenity, and produces constant stress that can shorten your life.

What takes the place of anxiety is the process of facing fear and feeling it, a process that unfolds something like this: When you're anxious, you go ahead and ask yourself, *What am I afraid of?* Once a fuzzy anxiety can be identified as a specific fear or cluster of fears, you tell fear, *I see you. I feel you. I'll figure out what your messages are. I'll keep acknowledging and confronting you as often as I must.*

With practice, this process produces calm. It becomes second nature, just as anxiety once was. But first you have to go through the anxiety of giving up anxiety.

Make Prayer a Habit

~

Pray without ceasing.

—1 THESSALONIANS 5:17

For many of us, prayer is a last resort. When we are afraid and desperately looking for a way to subdue fear, after all else has failed, we pray. Like Abraham Lincoln, we confess, "I have been driven many times to my knees by the overwhelming conviction that I had nowhere else to go." An alternative approach, one that's particularly useful in dealing with fear, is turning to prayer as *a constant resource,* making it the rule, not the exception. Viewed this way, prayer is a habit, something we simply do.

In his autobiography, the Dalai Lama, Tibet's exiled spiritual and political leader, mentions that he begins each day with, at the very least, five and a half hours of prayer, meditation, and study. Though this crusader for world peace who was honored with the 1989 Nobel Peace Prize has many responsibilities, he still finds time for regular, daily, spiritual practice.

What he shared next astounded me. Throughout the day, the Dalai Lama also fills spare moments with prayer because prayer "assuages fear!" That phrase and his exclamation point filled me with relief. Even the Dalai Lama, a wise and holy man, has to keep pacifying fear. Even he hasn't reached the pinnacle of fearlessness.

Though we too might like to use regular prayer to lessen our fear, what stops many of us is uncertainty. We wonder to whom we are directing our prayer. What are we supposed to say? Some of us no longer desire to connect with a childhood image of God. Sometimes the prayers we memorized when we were small no longer comfort us. So now how do we start over?

Benedictine monk Brother David Steindl-Rast spoke about a great mystic to whom God gave this message: "If you had not already found me, you would not be looking for me." The desire to pray is a deep awareness in our heart—even when our intellect is not convinced—that we don't have to remain separate from infinite wisdom, the divine within us or outside us. When we begin to pray, that power has already been found.

Endless debates about the "right" way to pray only delay our spontaneous prayers which are already *right*. We can say our prayers silently or out loud. We can sing them or chant them. We can petition God with specific requests: *Help me make it through all this. Show me what to do next. Thanks.* We can simply say, *Thy will be done.*

We can walk carefully, planting our feet on the ground in an attitude of reverence that uses no words at all. We can play our prayers on a musical instrument or let others' music move us to pray. Gradually, our repetitious prayers will become as comforting and natural as breathing—not a last resort, but a constant resource for facing fear.

Use Grown-Up Skills to Confront Fear

~

We need to realize that attitudes acquired earlier for
meeting childhood threats may turn out to be unsuited
to defend against adult dangers.

—SHELDON KOPP

When you find yourself feeling afraid, inadequate, and unable to face a situation that needs your courageous attention, this exercise may help you build your confidence. You can do this alone, but it's very comforting to have someone else, a mental health professional or a trusted friend, to accompany you.

Lie down or sit in a comfortable position. Close your eyes. Be open to recalling a particularly fearful event from your childhood and, when one appears, begin to observe the little girl or boy, not as if this little person is an earlier version of you, but as though she or he is a character in a movie.

Breathe deeply as you see this precious child in a scary situation. Be aware that the adult you is completely in control. If at any time what you see and hear becomes too frightening, stop, flip the switch, turn off the projector. If you want to go over a particular scene in more detail, freeze that frame, then go on.

I tried this with Marilyn, telling her: A ten-year-old girl is standing on a street corner on a warm spring evening. She's out on a walk with her parents. She's licking a chocolate ice cream cone. All day her stomach has been aching and now it feels as if molten lava flows through her abdomen. She's a compliant, quiet child and is hesitant to complain. But suddenly she has no choice. She throws the cone down and screams; her legs fold.

Her father scoops her up and carries her home. They get in the car and race to the hospital. Her appendix bursts as the doctor opens her up.

Now, remake the incident you observed, changing it any way you can imagine to help this child out. Give her or him a mature adult's insights and skills and ask, What could she or he do differently now?

Here's my revised story: Early in the day, the little girl tells the school nurse she's sick and goes home. She tells her mother she doesn't feel well and, as the pain gets worse, lets her mother know how bad it is. Her mother takes her to a doctor. He makes a diagnosis before the situation becomes critical.

Next, examine your story and ask yourself what lessons it holds that can help you right now. If none emerge, don't hurry the process. Days or weeks later something may trigger an "Oh, now I see." I reflect on how my parents could not read my mind. As a grownup, I see that I'm responsible for speaking up. I feel relieved. It's so obvious! Now when I face a threat of any sort, I can be assertive in seeking the exact type of assistance I need.

Repeat the exercise whenever you doubt your ability to face what you know you must. Different memories may come into your consciousness, or the same one may keep replaying. Be gentle with yourself. This exercise is not an excuse for self-flagellation. Rather, it is an opportunity to use reconstructive hindsight. As children, our repertoire of options was limited, our skills minimal. As adults, we can handle fearful situations with more awareness and confidence.

Ground Yourself in a Safe Spot

Find your own safe spots on the planet or in
your mind to sit with your fears.

—MARILYN SHROYER, PH.D.

At times, we must simply face our fears instantly, on the spot—any spot. But there are many other times when we can go to a special locale, a comfortable or inspiring place that makes us feel a little better just being there.

Do you have a place where you can sit with your fears and gather up your courage? When fear is making you feel disoriented, it's reassuring to have a few in mind. Even if circumstances keep you from going anywhere, you can construct special environments in your mind right where you are.

Do you feel drawn to mountains, forests, prairies, the ocean, a lake, or your backyard? Would you prefer to go to a library, a cafe, or a cathedral? For now, is your only choice your own bathroom, where you can at least lock the kids out?

I like to sit on a bench on the Fort Street Mall, a wide pedestrian-only street in downtown Honolulu. Last week when I was there, clusters of office workers were eating lunch, glancing at their watches. A Chinese college student on her way to classes at a nearby university expertly maneuvered her wheelchair around them. A couple of retired men with a bag of bread crumbs were surrounded by pigeons and doves. A bearded street person retrieved a half-full cup of Pepsi out of the trash. A band from the Andes was playing for donations, and a very drunk Joyce Brothers look-alike got up to perform a hula to the lively beat. Everyone clapped. I melt into humanity there, sensing that every person I see, for one reason or another, is in need of courage just as I am. In this setting, my concerns and fears don't vanish, yet somehow they seem more tolerable.

Marilyn lives in Denver, but at every opportunity she spends a few days or weeks at her little yellow clapboard house three blocks from the beach in Manzanita, Oregon. "I can more easily find the courage I need to face my fears when sitting on the beach," she explains. "The sound of the waves is soothing. My fears seem smaller when compared to the tremendous force of the ocean. Nature cuts them down to size, and I don't feel overwhelmed. Sometimes I write the names of my fears in the sand and watch the waves wash them away."

When you can't actually go someplace, you *can* go anyplace you want *in your mind*. To design your own secret inner space, relax and picture your mind as a blank white screen. Let an image of a safe environment arise to fill the screen. One woman visualized a room with white walls, a skylight, and no furnishings except a soft crimson oriental rug resting on a hardwood floor. She goes back there to feel her fears again and again. If she tires of this place, she has only to create a new one.

When you're feeling afraid, when you're needing courage, immerse yourself in a nurturing setting. Sink into your surroundings. Plant yourself there for a few minutes or for a few days. Pull up a chair, sit down on the ground, wade into the water, hike up a trail, or close your eyes. Whenever you need to, whenever you can, ground yourself in a safe spot.

Learn How to Live with Fear

⌒

To live with fear and not be afraid is the
final test of maturity.

—EDWARD WEEKS

Marilyn's grown daughter Michelle has lived with a kidney transplant from Marilyn for years. But recently, Michelle started showing serious signs of rejection.

Suddenly the low-level fear for her daughter that Marilyn has learned to live with turned into panic. "I wanted to jump out of my skin and escape somewhere," she remembers. "I've never been suicidal, but for a brief moment I wanted to get out of my life. I didn't have another kidney to give to Michelle—the helplessness and tension were more than I seemed to be able to bear."

With the help of a skilled medical team, the rejection process turned around—Michelle was going to be okay. Reflecting on almost losing her, Marilyn says, "I recognize that the Higher Power I pray to loves and cherishes Michelle as I do. It is very, very hard, but I'm working on affirming my trust in the universe, of being able to say, 'Thy will be done.' This growing trust has helped to calm my fears and even approach moments of peace."

A lot of situations like Michelle's tend to evoke fear again and again, and the fear will never totally disappear so long as the circumstances exist: Your former spouse is stalking you, and so far you haven't found any effective way to protect yourself; you're a paramedic, and your work regularly puts you in jeopardy; you quit a secure well-paying job with terrific health and retirement benefits to open your own business.

In these instances and many others, our challenge is not to banish fear forever but, as Marilyn is doing, to learn to live with it. Be firm with the fear that comes built into many situations, or it could become the roommate from hell, spreading its junk all over every single room in your mind, heart, body, and soul. Here are three suggestions to help:

Acknowledge the seriousness of your situation and the appropriateness of your fear. Keep reminding yourself, *My fear is natural. Of course I'm afraid—only a fool or an idiot wouldn't be.*

Speak up to fear and keep reminding it of your rules. Say, *I'd like to get rid of you. I know I can't, but I can keep you from walking all over me. You can't spill over into my entire life and take away my joy in being alive. Each time you try, I'll stop you.*

Know this: No matter how mature you become, no matter what you do, the fear you've been living with will sometimes burgeon into panic. When it does, be kind to yourself and reach for every resource possible. When Michelle was so ill, Marilyn called friends all over the country to pray for her. She didn't berate herself for feeling panicky; she flew to Michelle's bedside.

Though you cannot put fear like this permanently out on the street, you can confine it to a small basement room and keep it there most of the time.

Know That Risk Comes with the Territory

~

We cultivate fearlessness by being willing
to experience fear.

—STEPHEN LEVINE

When Natalie and Peter divorced, they ended a twelve-year union and broke up their business partnership. Much of the appeal of their two-person accounting firm had been that clients trusted both of them. Now Natalie was terrified many would simply take their business elsewhere. "I was taken to ground zero. I was devastated about the divorce. I'd lost my best friend and possibly my livelihood too. All my life I'd feared making it on my own. I wondered if I could survive emotionally or financially."

As Natalie was launching her own business, she lost so much weight that friends began to wonder if, in addition to everything else, she was seriously ill. For months she had to force herself to get out of bed and drag herself to work. For months she cried every night. When finally she fell asleep, she had nightmares about eating out of garbage cans and sleeping on park benches.

Finally, out of the chaos, Natalie's life began to take on a new shape. She retained some old clients and attracted new ones. She felt her confidence growing, and she knew she'd survive somehow, no matter how things turned out. In fact, her self-assurance bordered on euphoria. "As I began to cope, I started to feel fearless. I had survived the one thing I'd feared all my life. Now it seemed as if I'd never have to be afraid again."

Like Natalie, many of us believe that after we find the

courage to get through a very frightening experience, we've reached a high plateau, a special sacred place that's totally off limits to fear. We decide that fear is for beginners, not for pros like us who've already mastered it.

Natalie was shocked and disappointed to find out that going once through the refining fire victoriously had not granted her immunity from fear. Though she'd found courage she never imagined, soon old fears and insecurities began to pop up again, wearing different faces. As her business grew, she hired a new partner. Would this new woman work out? she worried. As time passed, she started dating again and found herself falling in love. Can I really allow myself to trust again? she kept asking herself. "It hardly seems fair, but I've come to see that there never comes a time when any of us can be totally free of fear so long as we live," Natalie reflects.

Certainly, it would be a lot easier if we could earn x number of courage points and then one day be exempt, totally free of fear once and for all. But in real life, this never happens. What is heartening, however, is that with practice, we really do get better at facing fear head-on. Instead of expending lots of energy trying to avoid it, we learn to face it sooner. We get more matter-of-fact about feeling it, more connected to the courage it takes to move through it. Rather than dwelling on catastrophe, we grow more confident that we will be able to face it. We can't eradicate fear. All we can do each time it arises is experience it. Once we know this, we can summon the courage for one more encounter. Feeling our fears each time they arise is the essence of fearlessness.

Find Fresh Approaches

On you will go/Onward up many/a frightening
creek,/though your arms may get sore/and
your sneakers may leak.

—DR. SEUSS

I don't know about you, but I can psych myself up for a one-time journey up a frightening creek—it's the repeated trips, the ones after my arms begin to ache and my sneakers begin to squish, that scare me. Unlike the Energizer bunny, I sometimes doubt I can keep on going and going, finding insights and energy again and again and again....

The truth is that many frightening situations are complex and ongoing. Consider, for instance, the following: You confront a coworker who is spreading gossip about you. You get through divorce proceedings with your integrity and dignity intact. You give a twenty-minute speech without shaking. You schedule an appointment with an OB/GYN specializing in infertility problems.

Tah dah! Hooray for me, you think, and rightly so. Then, with great relief, you say to yourself or a friend, "Well that's that!"

But life goes on. The coworker cries contrite tears, and the very next week lies about you again. The divorce is final, but your ex is unhappy with the settlement and keeps waking you at midnight with angry phone calls. Your professor assigns another speech, but this time it's ten minutes longer and you can't use notes. The medical procedures you hoped would help you get pregnant haven't worked after six long months.

As it often turns out, we don't always get to picnic and then plop down in a hammock near the creek's bank until we make many arduous journeys up many a frightening creek. And as we're forced into facing this reality, our original spark of courage may now give way to gray despair.

Besides sustaining enough stamina, the great challenge is that no two trips are alike—we can't rely on old remedies or fixed formulas. We can't really know exactly what we need to do until the current facts unfold. What worked last time may not apply in this newest slice of the saga. So we have to find the courage to keep climbing back into the boat in order to come to yet one more conclusion about how to handle our fears. Certainly, with our aching arms and soggy feet, we'd really rather not. But we must.

But first, renew yourself. Take a catnap or get a massage or go to a movie that transports you somewhere else. Meditate or pray. Cry. Scream. Pour out your woes to somebody you trust. Then dare to look carefully at what's going on this time. Size up the current dilemma, handling it as best you can. If it's any comfort, many of us have sore arms and wet sneakers—we're in the same boat.

Be Willing to Do the Hard Work of Courage

~

Courage is the price that life exacts for granting peace.

—AMELIA EARHART PUTNAM

It's such hard work, this trying to keep on. I'm tired. I don't have the courage to do it." Facing a divorce that may break him financially and major surgery that may not heal him, James expresses out loud what most of us think when we're in the middle of an especially terrifying period in our life.

Not one of us is eager to try on courage when what's happening to us is threatening us to the core. We're sure, under these extreme circumstances, that courage is way too hard for us. It makes us feel good to read about brave people who persevere through all kinds of horrendous things. It moves us to tears to see them on a movie screen. But as for claiming our own courage, we imagine we're just not up to it, and we'll have to do without it. Yet to find a measure of peace when we're in the middle of great difficulties, life exacts the very thing we're certain we can't manage: to be courageous. *Courage* comes from the French *coeur*, meaning heart. Courage is at the heart of our survival.

The problem is not that we *can't* be courageous, but that we decide not to. Courage is hard labor. It involves engaging in head-on confrontations with fear. It asks us to stop worrying so much—to start trusting that we can and will be okay, no matter what. It nudges us out of isolation to connect with people who can help. It won't shut up until we find sources of spiritual strength.

We can't purchase a season pass to courage, either. There's a daily price of admission we pay for with ongoing effort. And that can seem daunting. However, the truth is daunting, and we don't have many choices. We can take on the labor of courage, linger in an indecisive limbo, or choose the living hell of giving up, of saying, "I just can't do it."

There's no elevator up to courage. To get to it, we must make the ascent ourselves. If, right now, you're ready to quit climbing, first try this: *Picture three brave individuals— Grandpa, a friend, a speaker you heard at an AA meeting— anyone whose courage really touched you. Think about what each is or was up against. Write, call, or get together if you can, and ask, "How did you handle what you did?" or, "How are you keeping on now?" If you can't make contact, recall what this person said and how he or she acted when times were rough.* When you feel that you "just can't do it," let those who have, by their examples, help show you how.

All courage starts out as fear. We transform fear into courage by day-to-day, even minute-by-minute, decisions to keep climbing while accepting inevitable stalls and setbacks. To dare to take just the next step up is to embrace life and, at times, to feel an incredible peace within that has nothing at all to do with external circumstances.

We can, we must, do this impossible thing. If we carry on, tomorrow or in ten years, someone as scared as we are now—a son or a daughter, a friend, a colleague, or someone we met seemingly by chance and spoke with only once—will borrow some of our strength to keep on climbing.

Keep Making Brave Efforts

Oh Lord, thou givest us everything,

at the price of an effort.

—LEONARDO DA VINCI

Cultivating courage takes effort—not the frantic, sporadic kind, but relaxed, daily, even hourly effort. This week, to strengthen the habit of "doing" courage, here are suggestions for each day:

SUNDAY: *Do three things you fear.* Laziness, procrastination, and indecision are often fear in disguise. We're afraid we won't do something right, that we'll never catch up anyway, that trying something new will make us look foolish. Stop worrying about results and simply focus on *doing.* Write a note of apology you've been putting off. Clean out one desk drawer. Sign up for a class.

MONDAY: *Learn to breathe like a baby.* Lie on your back, placing one hand lightly on your belly. As you inhale, can you feel your abdomen rise, making your hand go up a little? As you exhale, do you feel your hand sinking back down? Infants breathe like this. But as we start holding tension and fear in our bodies, we get into the habit of taking shallow breaths or holding our breath. Become aware of your breathing and keep practicing until breathing like this begins to feel natural. Practicing courage is easier when we're relaxed and breathing easily.

TUESDAY: *Begin collecting courage-inspiring quotes.* Put them on the refrigerator door. Start a "courage" folder or computer file. Record a tape of the quotes and add your responses to them. In writing this book, I keep coming across gems like this one from Gabriele Rico: "'I can't' often means 'I won't.'"

WEDNESDAY: *Stop striving to become fearless.* No book, workshop, or pep talk will make all our fears vanish. Sometimes we have to go on living with fear because it's based on realistic concerns. If your fourteen-year-old has run away, of course you're afraid. If you're on your own for the first time, far from family and friends, especially in the beginning, this can be scary. Keep reminding yourself how courageous you are to keep facing your fears.

THURSDAY: *Complete this exercise devised by psychotherapist Richard Frank: If I had infinite courage, I would.... If I were an infinite coward, I would....* Pour out as many responses to both as you can think of, writing down anything that comes to mind. The first sentence can help you become aware of what you're afraid of so you can summon more courage in these areas. It's fun, in the second one, to turn into the consummate coward on paper *and* to see that you're not really as big a wimp as you sometimes think.

FRIDAY: *Pick out a few courage symbols.* What might you wear or have around that would help you relax and claim your courage? An old flannel shirt? A baseball cap? A quilt your grandmother made? When my sons were little, they gave me a pewter turtle on a chain. Wearing it made me feel more courageous. I felt a spiritual connection with the slowpoke turtle and began collecting little turtle figures and turtle jewelry.

SATURDAY: *Encourage others.* Send someone a cartoon, note, or inspiring quote. Deliver a fruit basket. Keep a friend's kids for a day. Share details of your experience with someone who may be thinking, I'm the only one who struggles like this. Listen to others' fears with a quiet mind and no ready advice—just listen.

Step into the Darkness to Find the Light

~

AIDS may take my body but I refuse
to give it my spirit.

—CHELSIE

Ven E. Sipe spent most days at Bailey-Boushay House in Seattle, a residential care facility for people with AIDS. There, this intense, articulate young man talked with me one April afternoon. He was eager to share his experiences so I could pass them on to you.

"We're a tribe, all of us," he began. "What one individual has experienced can help another. We all have fears, and we can learn from hearing about how others face theirs."

Then Ven told me about a ritual that was helping him hold on to his spirit. "Once a week, at night, I walk barefoot through the woods. When I'm standing at the edge of the forest, it's very scary. All I can see is darkness, and I wonder what I'm going to step into. But once I'm inside, I don't see black but shades of shadows and shapes of trees. I've stepped through the darkness. There is nothing to be afraid of in there, and the fear washes away."

Again and again, through this ritual, Ven acknowledged his fear and stepped into it. "You have to check to see where the roots of each fear are coming from," he said. "You have to breathe with fear. It won't go away until you master it."

A Chinese proverb says, "You can go only halfway into the darkest forest; then you are coming out the other side." What Ven told me resonated with that wisdom: We're required to enter our dark fears over and over; plant our bare feet on the earth; breathe in and out consciously; and walk past our fears and see their shades and shapes, recognizing them as part of us, just as joy and laughter are.

Later I mailed Ven a litany against fear from the science fiction classic Dune by Frank Herbert: "Fear is the mind-killer. Fear is the little-death that brings total obliteration. I will face my fear. I will permit it to pass over me and through me. And when it has gone past I will turn the inner eye to see its path. Where the fear has gone there will be nothing. Only I will remain."

When Ven wrote back, he said, "I am so sick and tired of all of these deaths. It seems every week there is someone that I know, or someone close to me knows, who just died. AIDS AIDS AIDS!!! When will there be a cure?" And finally, he reflected, "I spend more time counting my blessings rather than counting my losses. I spent most of the month in bed, so I now know the everyday sounds here very well. . . . I give you my support and encouragement in the process of writing this book."

In the fall of 1993, Ven passed away. AIDS took his body, but he lived with dignity and courage, refusing to give it his spirit. He signed that last letter to me "Your eternal friend." By sharing with me and with you, Ven's a friend who left permanent, specific instructions about how to walk straight into any dark and terrible fear: It looks totally black from the outside, but once you step in, there are shapes and shadows. It's not as scary once you've walked into the woods of your fears.

Transforming Fear

Unpleasant emotions such as fear are part of every human's existence. Again and again, every single day, we have opportunities to be with our fears and allow them to teach us. And when we do, we get tougher, stronger. We don't grow wings; we get callused hands and feet down here in the middle of it all. We climb out from under the covers, step into the day, bypass worry and anxiety, and go over to gratitude and wonder as often as we can. We keep seeing what's going on around us, keep feeling what's happening inside, and keep responding as best we can.

It makes no sense, but the more habitually we meet fears head-on like this, the more likely they are to become something entirely different. By facing and feeling our fears day after day, by transcending them with our humble efforts, sometimes they undergo a transformation. Just as we offer our fears even grudging acceptance, often they surprise us and actually change into such qualities as contentment, courage, compassion, love, faith, or calm awareness.

You can't count on this transformation. You can't force it. But when you keep facing your fears and feeling them, one of two miracles happens: You receive the grace to live with fear, or you witness fear turning into something new. Either way, be conscious of this: You cultivate courage and grow in integrity by facing and feeling each fear.

Claim the Courage That's Already Yours

~

Before dropping off to sleep, I would imagine
myself being charged with courage, because oh, how I
needed courage, and I knew courage was the antithe-
sis of fear. I had learned not to plead and yammer,
"Oh God, take away this fear," but to say firmly
instead, "I have courage," and I would imagine
I could actually see it pouring down into my
sleeping body, burning up the fears in my
mind, filling it with new life.

—CATHERINE COOKSON

Imagine this: You have to go out into a cold, driving rain, but you've lost your umbrella. You search everywhere, but it still doesn't turn up. You start to get uneasy. Then along comes a funny kind of miracle. You see that you couldn't find your umbrella because you never really lost it—it was dangling from your wrist by a sturdy knotted loop all along. You just got so caught up in imagining your teeth chattering and your clothes plastered against your skin that you lost all awareness of its presence. Now you open up your umbrella and step outside confidently.

Courage is like this. It's yours to open up and use during a life storm by becoming aware that you have it. Then when you need it, you can affirm the fact of your ownership by simply saying *I have courage!* When you're very frightened, this may sound absurd, but it's not. To *affirm* literally means "to make firm." Especially when you're shaky and unsure of yourself, it helps to validate the reality of your courage. Even when fear is taking up most of the space in your mind, courage is waiting for you to call it out of a dark corner.

When you say, *I have courage!* you are announcing your intention to affirm the very core of yourself. You are reaching deep inside to discern what your highest course is. Then by some grace you may never fully understand, you can begin to walk on the path that courage shows you and keep coming back anytime you stray from it.

Though claiming courage is not easy, it has deep rewards. In *The Courage to Be,* theologian Paul Tillich writes, "The affirmation of one's essential being in spite of desires and anxieties creates joy." When we dare to affirm our essence, to be open to growing up and going on, courage begins to displace fear, and joy and relief accompany our conscious choices. We can say to ourselves, for instance, *I'm not sure how I'm going to survive financially, but I'm glad I quit my job when I found out how shoddy the company's products were. I left feeling like a million dollars.*

Use the statement *I have courage!* as often as you need to. Then at bedtime, as Catherine Cookson described, imagine courage pouring down into your body, burning up the fears in your mind. Breathe deeply and consciously, enjoying the spaciousness of a mind that, for now, is cleared of all fear and ready for a good night's sleep.

Affirming your courage won't dislodge ingrained patterns of fearful thinking overnight. But by building this habit, gradually you will learn to stop fearing fear and to keep facing and feeling every single fear that you have. You don't have to plead for courage—it's yours. All you have to do is bravely claim it again and again.

Find One Reason to Go On

~

You must go on, I can't go on, I'll go on.

—SAMUEL BECKETT

How long has it been since you had an internal dialogue like the one above? Five years or only a few minutes ago? When you fear you simply can't go on and you fantasize about driving off in any direction, so long as it's far away, what might keep you from giving up?

What happened to Anna Marie Tesoriero on February 26, 1993, illustrates how sometimes with no warning we may be forced into finding an answer. That day, when she took her kindergarten class on an outing at the World Trade Center in Manhattan, a terrorist bomb devastated the building. For five hours, they were trapped in the dark in a hot, smoky elevator on the thirtieth floor.

Anna Marie, claustrophobic and afraid of the dark, began hyperventilating and felt an anxiety attack coming on, but she was able to quell her fears by deciding she simply could not let the children down. Telling her story in *Ladies Home Journal*, she explained how she stopped thinking about herself or even of her family: "All I thought about was the children; I had to get them through it."

Whether we are caught in a terrifying ordeal, want to meet a challenge but are doubting we're up to it, or face day-in-and-day-out difficulties that are wearing us out, it's crucial to latch onto any positive incentives we can think of to keep going. Sometimes very small pleasures help. A housewife who dreads waking up, having to remember all over again that she lost a breast to cancer and faces months of chemotherapy, started a morning ritual of leisurely sipping a cup of Earl Grey tea and reading the comic strips before tackling anything else. A man, struck down by a drunk driver while crossing the street, escapes with Douglas Adams's science fiction novels while he's recuperating from multiple painful injuries. "I read about the absurdities of life and I have a laugh," he says.

Often what helps is an opportunity to help somebody else. A mother whose six-year-old son drowned in a freak accident in the Gulf of Mexico finds solace in spearheading a citizens' action group to educate the public on beach safety. A widow, feeling very lonely after her mate of forty years passed away, is smiling again. Her grandson, just out of college, got a new job not far from her and needed a place to live. When she offered him a room and bath "cheap," plus home-cooked dinners, he accepted.

You can't always alter a situation or escape it. You can't always find a good reason for why you're in a particular predicament in the first place. But you can transform the fear that you can't go on into courage that moves you forward. Joy and meaning can sneak back into your life as you begin to let yourself experience small pleasures and find ways to show your concern for others.

There must be a million reasons to go on, but we need to start by finding only one or two. If you are too depressed to think of a single one, brainstorm with an upbeat and encouraging person. Rent an inspiring movie such as the Jimmy Stewart classic *It's a Wonderful Life*. And whatever else you do, *relax*—it will take time, but by being open to going on, possibilities that were hidden from you before will begin to reveal themselves.

Dig for the Sources of Your Fears

As soon as we understand the causes and nature of our
feelings, they begin to transform themselves.

—THICH NHAT HANH

A couple of years ago, after her third divorce, Marilyn faced her addiction to relationships. Part of her ongoing recovery program is attending a twelve-step support group. Recently while working on the ominous-sounding fourth step, the one that involves making "a searching and fearless moral inventory," she began to write down her fears. "I was surprised," she says, "to find myself putting down, 'I'm afraid I'll remain a shallow lover.'"

As memories welled up, Marilyn began to understand more about the causes and nature of this particular fear. "When I was eleven, I liked to put a nickel into a vending machine in the Ben Franklin variety store near my house to get a fortune. I've forgotten all of them except one: '*You will be married nine times.*' This horrified me as I thought about how this would surely humiliate my family.

"This memory became more powerful when coupled with later events. In my teens, when I was in tears after my latest beau broke my heart, my dad would try to comfort me with one of his favorite sayings: 'Men are like buses—another one will be along in five minutes.' During my adolescence, it seemed Dad was right. I had a whole series of boyfriends. *Easy come, easy go* best describes these immature relationships that offered a lot of excitement and glitz to make up for a nonnurturing family life. My relationship addiction grew out of these early experiences. My drug of choice became men—plural.

"All addictions stall growth, and mine kept me from evolving into a mature lover. I never learned how to accept the inevitable weaknesses of others. My ability to admit and confront my own inadequacies was in an atrophied state. I kept trading partners, believing the next one would be 'the right bus.'

"My greatest fear is that I'll keep settling for the surface excitement and glamour of revolving love affairs without going through the pain of forming a deep relationship. By facing my fear head-on, I understand its roots better. I see how I've habitually escaped when the going got rough in relationships."

Now that Marilyn knows her fear this well, now that she understands its origins, it no longer holds as much power over her. "I believe my fear can finally begin to shrink and transform itself into the courage to try out new ways of relating. I want to learn to love generously and to allow myself to be loved."

Once we understand the causes and nature of our fears, we free them to undergo a major change in form and function—we release them to transform themselves. Though such transformations sound mystical, they are not. They happen when we stop hoping for miracles and start doing the demanding, sometimes frightening work required to understand what caused a fear to lodge in our heart in the first place. Alone or with the help of a therapist, trusted friend, or support group, our efforts can finally help us send this fear on its way.

Get Furious with Fear

~

Now he'll outstare the lightning. To be furious
is to be frightened out of fear.

—SHAKESPEARE

Donald, a precocious five-year-old, struggles with a pervasive fear of just about everything—the dark, his new day care center, even clouds. For instance, when he's out playing t-ball, he looks up at a few wispy clouds and imagines them billowing into fierce thunderheads. And then he pictures a bolt of lightning obliterating him.

When Donald gets this frightened, there's no way he can focus on the game or have fun with his teammates. He is terrified of his fear and terribly afraid that it's going to ruin his life. This is making him really furious. The first time he came for therapy with Marilyn, he begged her, "Don't let my fear interfere with me!" Later he used this phrase as a chant to help him gather courage.

Often when we're afraid, we feel depressed and immobilized. But in that depression, there is a spark of fury that we can put to use as Matthew did. *Furiosus,* the Latin word from which *fury* is derived, means "full of madness or rage." In my 1908 Latin-English dictionary, I found nine more closely related Latin words, all packed with action. For instance, the *Furies* were three raging and dreadful goddesses of vengeance. Persons who are furious resemble them in that they too are bent on retaliation.

The challenge, when we're furious with our fears and frightened that they are interfering with our life, is deciding how to move out of passive resignation into active participation in subduing them. What exactly is our best revenge?

Karen, who had ovarian cancer, found a way to plot revenge from her hospital bed. She and her husband, Anthony, had asked her doctor not to give her any more negative statistics or predictions. She was afraid one more bit of bad news would take away her will to go on. She and Anthony made it clear to her doctor that they'd prefer he pass on any such information to Anthony, who would then sort out what he thought Karen really needed to know.

But one day Karen's doctor walked into her room, asked her friends to step outside, and said to her, "You need to prepare yourself to die very soon." Karen cried, shivered in fright, and then she got furious—he had just broken the rules. She told Anthony, and together they fired the doctor. The next day their new physician began their alliance by telling her, "Several things could be happening. We don't want to assume the worst."

In a week, Karen felt well enough to leave the hospital. She and Anthony spent a romantic Christmas together in a log cabin in the Rockies, and Karen lived for many more precious months.

Whatever is frightening you, go ahead and dare to outstare the lightning. Don't let your fear interfere with you. Use your fury for fuel. Let it move you out of fear.

Puʃh Paʃt Fear

~

Feel the fear and do it anyway.

—SUSAN JEFFERS, PH.D.

I have a forty-year-old friend who finally got up the courage to go skydiving for the first time. She runs a catering business and loves it, but she wanted a day away from making little pinwheel sandwiches and browning mini-meatballs. She knew she needed a glimpse of the bigger picture and thought skydiving might restore her perspective. It did: "I felt an immense gratitude for everything—the earth below and my body soaring above it. You know how I did it?" she giggled. "I tipped the instructor an extra twenty bucks to shove me out of the plane!"

Some of us might have to have a gun at our heads before we'd try skydiving, but all of us have some big or little things we really want or need to do but keep putting off until we master our fears. And so we tell ourselves, *I'll speak up to my dad about how angry I feel each time he puts me down—as soon as I get up the nerve . . . I'll keep working behind the scenes to preserve the historical district, but I'm just too shy to be interviewed by the media . . . I'll visit Aunt Ella after I get over my dread of going into nursing homes . . . One day soon I'll take my paintings by the gallery to see if they might be interested in displaying them.*

There's no reason to confront and conquer everything we're afraid of. For many people, for instance, there is great fun in forever skiing down intermediate hills, never finding out how big the moguls are on the expert runs. But when fear stifles our sense of adventure—stopping us from doing acts of kindness, making us stay quiet when we need to speak up, undermining our ability to use our gifts and talents, keeping us from living by the values we hold—we need to push on through it, even with wobbly knees, a pounding heart, or a quivering voice.

My son Matt likes the research he's involved in. But to stay in school, be paid for his work, and eventually earn a Ph.D. in chemical oceanography, he has to do more than go out in the ocean on research vessels, collect data, and bring it back to the laboratory to analyze. He's also required to give talks before other students, present papers to the scientific community, and teach undergraduate classes.

For years, any kind of public speaking stirred up debilitating fear in Matt, not merely stage fright that spoiled the day of the speech, but fear that took over weeks ahead. Because he wants to complete his degree, he decided to keep feeling his fear and speaking anyway. For a long time, he overprepared for each speech, joking, "If I'm going to be scared, I may as well be prepared." Finally, his perseverance is paying off. Now he experiences only prespeaking jitters and likes teaching enough to consider it as a career option. Should he totally change his mind about his life work, he'll take his confidence along to any new setting.

Keep in mind that feeling the fear and doing it anyway is not about impressing or pleasing anyone or about casually rushing into dangerous situations. Only you can decide when to override your fears. Look carefully at what you're taking on and proceed with a healthy respect for the fear you're facing and for yourself.

Turn and Face Your Shadow

~

Real safety lies in your willingness not to
run away from yourself.

—DAWNA MARKOVA, PH.D.

The little story that follows is attributed to Chuang Tzu, the great Taoist philosopher who lived around 250 B.C. Once there was a man who got so upset by the sight of his own shadow and was so unhappy with his own footsteps that he tried to run from both. But each time his foot hit the ground, he realized he was still taking a step. Equally disturbing, he saw that his shadow never once fell behind. Not about to give up, he ran faster, faster, faster until finally he dropped dead. What he never grasped was that by stepping into the shade, his shadow would vanish. By simply sitting down, there would be no more footsteps.

Like the man in this story, many of us are terrified of what lurks in our shadow yet aware that running away from it is exhausting us. According to Jung's theory of the shadow, hidden in the unconscious are all the aspects of ourselves we do not know we possess. They're like unused items that were put away in a trunk in the basement and forgotten.

To run from what we don't know about ourselves, and to resist new knowledge about who we really are, is an automatic response. To dare to stop, to sit in the shade and survey what's there, is a conscious act of courage.

This doesn't mean we feel courageous when we embark on this exploration. Usually we're simply too tired to keep running. This is also not to say that this journey into ourselves is easy. It involves taking off our masks, finding out what real beliefs lie beneath the mottoes we've memorized, glimpsing and releasing long-suppressed rage, and acknowledging talents we never unwrapped and used. Letting go of preconceived notions we had about ourselves is frightening but ultimately liberating. In our shadows are dormant ideas and inclinations waiting to be dusted off and used—as well as tendencies to beware of.

If you knew you had just three months to live, what would you do differently? Stop letting your spouse slap you around? Learn to fly? Gather your kids and grandkids around and just play? Begin saying what you *really* think? Run up all your credit cards to their limits? Eat all the death-by-chocolate desserts you want? Honestly answering this question can shed more light on your shadow, so let your responses tumble out without censoring or judging them.

Once we begin to look at dark parts we were afraid to claim before, we discover rewards for gaining more self-knowledge. When we make an ongoing commitment to continue discovering and accepting all that's within us, we start to make friends with our quirks and oddities, our hidden strengths, as well as our mean and hateful tendencies. We no longer feel like bearing arms against ourselves or anybody else. It occurs to us that we can lay down our weapons and open our arms to a world that, like us, is rich and complex.

The way we treat ourselves is the way we treat our world. The more fear and prejudice we aim at parts of ourselves, the more fear and prejudice we project onto others. Out of the peace we make with ourselves we find insights and strength to make contributions toward peace in our home, our neighborhood, and the world.

Tap into Your Own Brand of Courage

~

All acts of courage communicate the
same message: "This is me!"

—ROBERT J. FUREY, PH.D.

Sometimes we wish that deciding how to express our courage were as simple as completing a paint-by-number canvas. To be courageous, all we'd have to do is buy somebody else's representation, accept the palette they chose, and dab the right colors in the right spaces. But acts of real courage never come out of easy-to-follow kits; they arise and take shape deep within our hearts. Each authentic expression of courage is an original canvas, an attitude or act that has never been visualized and taken form in quite the same way—a glimpse of the divine in us.

All of us can be great artists, courageous enough to express our inner visions. But first we need to stop focusing on getting approval from others and approve ourselves. Some people may notice and applaud our courage; others won't. We will never find our own special courage so long as we base our decisions on how much attention, affirmation, or admiration we will be likely to receive.

Another obstacle to finding our unique courage is a desire to define courage once and for all. There simply is no single, inclusive formula. Each time we face a challenge, we have to make a courageous decision based on new circumstances. It helps to remember times in the past when we were courageous and to remind ourselves that we can be courageous once again. But what worked last year, even last month, may not work now. Only by giving careful attention to what's happening right now can we make one more courageous decision.

Sometimes courage asks us to find the patience of a lei maker, carefully stringing one little blossom after another. Sometimes it demands that we say, "I can't stay in this situation one minute longer!" Sometimes courage means pouring lots of time into projects to help save the planet. Sometimes it whispers, "Pull back for a while and teach your children how to plant a garden." Sometimes courage reminds us that keeping up a big home is leaving little time to grow spiritually. Sometimes it asks us to add another room to the house so Grandma can live with us. Sometimes courage urges us to accept our poverty and remain in school to earn the piece of paper that will allow us to follow our dream. Sometimes it shows us that our path requires no more formal education, that we need to get out of classrooms and into the world to design our own curriculum.

The only constant requirement of courage is that it emanate from the most loving, essential part of yourself. Throw away all other rules. Stop dreaming of applause. Don't be afraid to tap into your own brand of courage—your courage isn't like anybody else's.

Find Joy in Life "As Is"

Those who can most truly be accounted brave
are those who best know the meaning of what is
sweet in life and what is terrible, and then go out,
undeterred, to meet what is to come.

—PERICLES

For many years, Sarah Shanahan, now in her late forties, was the proverbial superwoman—a mother of two, wife, and flight attendant, who on days "off" did volunteer work, ran a small business, concocted gourmet meals, kept an immaculate home, and worked out regularly. What used to sweeten life for this slender woman with big, intense eyes and a curly mane of long brown hair was managing to juggle all this. What used to be terrible, she recalls, was being constantly afraid she'd drop one of the balls. "I felt worthless if I wasn't larger than life."

What happened on February 24, 1989, permanently revised her outlook. As the United flight was climbing to cruising altitude after taking off from Honolulu past midnight, a cargo door opened, ripped loose, and tore a big gaping hole in the fuselage. In a terrible instant, nine passengers were sucked out of the plane into the darkness. Then the number three engine failed and number four caught fire. As the captain turned the severely damaged jetliner back to Honolulu, Sarah was sure they were all going to die. Amazingly, twenty interminable minutes later, he landed safely. Sarah, a twelve-year veteran, efficiently directed relieved passengers down emergency chutes.

After four months off, Sarah was back at work, convinced she'd put the horror behind her, but on a layover a few weeks later, she had a total breakdown. The belief that held her together before, the notion that we can control life if only we remain smart enough and vigilant enough, had been obliterated by scary new indelible realities. "You never know what corner death's lurking around. What life is about is the possibility of being dead tomorrow."

Before going back to work again, Sarah entered therapy, facing her rage and terror that life can suddenly, randomly be taken away. She felt foolish "for buying the myth of control for so long."

Today, Sarah is still a flight attendant, but she's no longer juggling so many balls. She says now she just enjoys "tossing one up in the air." The tragedy, plus an assortment of other experiences, could have left her permanently angry and resentful. But she's not because she's aware now that holding on to these unpleasant emotions is not her only choice.

Sarah tells a Hawaiian story to illustrate her point: "Once a little girl was given a beautiful bowl of light. Out walking one day, she started picking up black rocks, dropping one after the other into the bowl until it got so heavy that she began to have trouble going on. Now she was faced with a decision—to dump out all the rocks and go on with a light-filled bowl, or to be weighted down by the dark burdensome load."

Sarah's conclusion is this: It's not worth it to keep lugging around heavy dark rocks because life is sometimes tragic and often not exactly as we'd like it. Still, even knowing better, our human tendency is to forget and pick up one more dark load. And so it's up to us to bravely discard whatever is there, again and again, slowly building a new habit of traveling lightly and joyfully.

Under∧tand the Di∬erence
Between World and Succe∧∧

~

Try not to become a person of success,

but rather a person of value.

—ALBERT EINSTEIN

S ix-year-old Benjamin Petrosuis tried out for the starring role in *Dennis the Menace,* made it all the way into a small circle of nine finalists, but was not chosen. When asked how he felt, he told *Premiere* magazine, "I'm trying to get my life back together."

We can all identify with the disappointment of trying hard for something and not getting it. But at any age—six or sixty—when the glue that holds life together is landing a star role, gaining professional success, or achieving a certain standard of living, we can end up living in constant fear. If where we work, how much we earn, or what our address is determines our worth, we know that one day we could be "successful," but the next day we could loose it all.

It's stressful to live like this, yet so many of us do. When we interviewed people in their teens and twenties about what they feared, most mentioned, in one context or another, "not making it." One sixteen-year-old imagined himself "flipping hamburgers for a living forever." A twenty-seven-year-old college graduate, who worked in an office and was saving for graduate school, doubted she'd go to her tenth high school reunion because she wasn't "successful yet."

Where does our obsession with success come from? Some of our parents made it clear that they expected us to "amount to something," to enter professions worth bragging about. Many, sold on achieving success themselves, truly wanted "the best" for us too. But even if our own parents didn't emphasize success above all else, we all live in a society that does.

In the mail yesterday, I got a glossy reminder of this mindset—an offer to buy a set of audio cassettes about how to achieve success. Their creator, I read, had been broke, alone, and living in a dumpy little apartment just six years before. But now, after tapping into some amazing principles, he had multi-million bucks, a wife and kids, and a mansion with five-digit square footage.

It's a reality that we need enough income for basic living expenses. And we all long to find work that allows us to express our talents and training. But it's unnatural and debilitating to measure our value by outward standards of success such as those outlined in his story. It was easy to toss this into the trash, but it's not always easy to junk ingrained ways of thinking about what constitutes a person of value.

Why are you valuable? Consider this uncomplicated answer: *We all are valuable simply because we are alive.* After acknowledging and claiming our inherent worth, we can relax, take our time, and be open to finding ways to make our unique contributions to the world. It doesn't matter nearly so much what anybody thinks, once we start to know our own value and feel it deep in our bones. That basic act of kindness toward ourselves is a firm foundation from which to construct a life of kindness and compassion for our world.

Want What You Have

~

Happiness is less a matter of getting what we
want than wanting what we have.

—DAVID G. MYERS, PH.D.

M any of us live with the nagging fear that we'll never have
quite all the right ingredients on hand to complete the
recipe for a happy life. Though we don't usually throw a public
tantrum, when listening to our private thoughts we often hear a
little kid whining, *More! MORE!* or, *Not THAT one, I wanted
the OTHER one,* or, *Get this awful-looking green stuff off my
plate. Gimme a bowl of chocolate ice cream (that won't make
me fat), and then I'll settle down and be happy.*

But what if we *do* get what we want? Will that make us
happy? What if Ed McMahon shows up at our front door,
telling us we're the big sweepstakes winner? Or we marry the
most wonderful person on earth? Or we move into a mansion
with walk-in closets? Or we inherit a fortune, quit our job, and
move to Bora Bora to write the great American novel? Or we
wake up one morning miraculously cured of arthritis or
asthma?

In *The Pursuit of Happiness,* David Myers writes, "The
consistent finding from dozens of studies is that objective life
experiences, once we've adapted to them, bear little relation to
people's happiness." In other words, when something we perceive as good fortune actually comes our way, our happiness
level shoots up, and our fear of not getting "it" plummets.
We're euphoric or at least a little more satisfied for a while. But
it's like eating a brownie or drinking a Coke. Once the tempo-
rary high wears off, invariably, we fall right back into the habit-
ual level of happiness we're used to.

Conversely, when we face a disaster or loss, happiness plummets and we feel afraid, depressed, sad, or angry for a time. But even after a tornado rips the roof off our house, a loved one dies, or we become disabled or terminally ill, typically we eventually return to the level of happiness that we've habitually cultivated.

If you're tired of never finding the happiness that lies out there just ahead and afraid it's beginning to look as though you never will, this is a perfect time to practice the art of unconditional happiness. Here's how to begin: Every morning when you wake up, say to yourself, *I am very lucky to be alive.* (Or use *fortunate* or *blessed* if it suits you better.) During the day, each time you start resenting your circumstances or begin feeling sorry for yourself, say it again. Especially if you wake up in the middle of the night, repeat this phrase. Even though it may feel phony and you're positive you're not lucky at all, keep repeating it for weeks or months and one day you'll see—the "poor me" story line you were convinced was truth was, in reality, fiction.

Having to have something, being convinced we can't be satisfied until *x* happens, causes chronic fear and obscures our vision so much that we can't see the good things right in front of us. Nothing we *get* can make us permanently happy. Nothing we *lose* has to make us permanently unhappy. All of us have the capacity to choose to be happy no matter what happens or doesn't happen. Once we claim that power, we're free to start concocting happiness out of anything we have on hand. All of us are truly lucky to have what we have, which, at the very least, is the miraculous breath of life.

Give Yourself Permission to Be Human

~

We must learn to give ourselves permission to
blunder, to fail, and to make fools of ourselves
every day for the rest of our lives.

—SHELDON KOPP

One of the keys to transforming fear is to give ourselves permission to make mistakes. Many of us are afraid that no matter how hard we try we will never get everything quite right. It seems like we gain knowledge and expertise, even wisdom, in one area only to have new challenges come along that remind us we can still be clumsy, inept, silly, and unenlightened.

Though mistakes can embarrass or even humiliate us, they are our best tutors. Instead of fearing them, instead of asking life for a less demanding instructor, we can stop trying to maintain a flawless image and start trying new things, no matter how well we do them. We can give ourselves permission to blunder, to fail, and to make fools of ourselves.

Sean, a musician in his midtwenties, expresses how this works for him. He used to drink excessively to escape his feelings but has been sober for six years. For five years, he's had a regular meditation practice. "It would be nice to meditate for a while and come up with some great realization, and from that point on have my life be whole. But that hasn't happened. My path hardly has grace. It's not as obvious as when I was drinking. Now I embarrass myself and hurt myself in a lot of subtle ways. I have to have these really painful ego-puncturing experiences to help me grow.

"Mistakes are food for growth," Sean continues. "A lot of

masterpieces were created by a mistake. A painter may reach to his palette and think he's getting blue, but gets red, mixes that with some other color, and makes a new shade he never found before. If I have a bad gig, it can be a motivating force for me to gain new understanding about my playing or myself."

Learning to let ourselves make mistakes is a crucial fear-transforming skill. Here are six guidelines:

1. Stop agonizing, *Will I make a mistake?* So long as you keep engaging yourself in life, you bet you will. So relax, this is one thing you can count on.

2. Remember: At least five mistakes a day will keep pride away. If you always did everything flawlessly, you might become arrogant. If you're not making a few mistakes each day, it may be just because you're avoiding any challenges.

3. Make fresh mistakes. Don't keep repeating the same old ones. For example, after approximately the twentieth time that I locked my keys in the car, I finally stopped. My simple solution: I never slam the door before first asking myself, *Do I have the keys?*

4. When you make a really big mistake that hurt you or someone else, you may never entirely forget, but you can forgive yourself and learn from it. Preoccupation with the past won't change what happened and keeps you from being fully present now.

5. Let your mistakes originate from good intentions. Make mistakes while you're giving full attention to loving, learning, and attending to what needs to be done.

6. When, inevitably, some of your mistakes flow out of arrogance, greed, anger, or prejudice, or because you were annoyed or spaced out, acknowledge their origins. Allow these mistakes you especially regret to teach you more compassion for yourself and all of humankind.

Follow Your Heart

⁓

When you rock the boat, someone will
tell you to sit down.

—SUSAN JEFFERS, PH.D.

hen you catch a glimpse of a dream and begin to gather the courage to go after it, it's natural to want to share this with family and friends. But not all of them will become cheerleaders. Some may even make fun of you and try their best to turn you back into the coward they knew and loved.

In the classic children's book *The Little Engine That Could*, to keep steaming up the hill, the little engine kept repeating, "I think I can. I think I can." We need to keep saying that to ourselves too. But many times loved ones do their best to drown that out with, "I doubt that you can. I wonder if you should." And this only feeds our fear more.

Recently, Marilyn's twenty-four-year-old daughter, Aimee, a hair stylist, decided she was ready to venture away from Denver, where she'd always lived. She dreamed of working in a salon aboard a cruise liner, visiting exotic ports, and meeting tourists from all over the world. She updated her résumé and was all prepared to mail out copies—that is, until she let family and friends in on her plans.

A few of their comments: "Zillions of others must be applying for these glamorous jobs. Why waste your time?" "The living quarters are too cramped. You'll never be happy without two closets full of clothes." "You won't have a phone, so how could the family stay in touch?" And the pièce de résistance: "Who do you think you are anyway? No one in this family has ever been on a cruise, not even for a vacation!"

Mulling all this over, Aimee's enthusiasm turned to fear.

Obviously, it must have been a stupid idea, she reasoned. At this point, Marilyn, who was cheering her daughter on, encouraged her: "Don't give up—get more information." After tracking down a reliable source acquainted with the cruise industry, Aimee found out answers to questions she had, plus those that concerned others. Quarters are cramped, but the food is terrific. Many applicants get turned down, but with her advanced training, she had a good chance. Pay is low—tips are great. Staying in contact is not a problem.

Now, with an accurate idea of what she'd be getting into, Aimee decided that she still wanted the job, so she mailed out ten résumés. In less than a month, a Hawaii-based cruise line offered her a job, and she was off.

If you are attempting to turn a dream into reality and are trying to maintain enough courage to do it, consider these wise words from Clarissa Pinkola Estes: "When seeking guidance, don't ever listen to the tiny-hearted. Be kind to them, heap them with blessing, cajole them, but do not follow their advice."

Our dreams to go far away or simply to behave in a new way sometimes stir fear and insecurity in those close to us. It's up to us to make our own informed decision, then to do all the hard work it takes to journey to a new place. If you can, find at least one fellow dreamer who will encourage you. Then send all the rest postcards from exotic places on the globe or from bright new places in your heart.

Transform Fear into Art

~

The only way I get rid of my fears is
to make films about them.

—ALFRED HITCHCOCK

Recently, I read about sculptor Nancy Fried, who after her mastectomy began to depict her experience in clay. In one piece, a woman is crying, holding her severed breast. To turn our fears into artistic expressions is a powerful, healing way to transform them. It can be very satisfying to take shapeless, chaotic fears and harness their power, channeling it into new forms.

For five years, I taught an ongoing creative writing class at Mountain Vista Nursing Home in Wheat Ridge, Colorado. Often students turned their inmost fears into stories, essays, and poems. Here are three topics they explored:

- Turn yourself into a piece of furniture.
- Become a road—a dirt path, a superhighway, any kind.
- Choose an animal that best symbolizes you and tell about life as if you are the animal.

Try these yourself, using the first person: "I am a...." If you'd prefer, draw, paint, photograph, or sculpt them.

When Verna Rinne, a widow, mother of two, and formerly a homemaker, joined the class, she was in her seventies and had severe arthritis. That didn't stop her from becoming a writer. I've lost track of how many of her poems and essays were published. She wrote for as long as she could grasp a pen. Finally, her fingers became too crippled and weak.

Here are excerpts from one of the last pieces she wrote before she died. She had to dictate her words:

I am a rocking chair, old, my arms worn smooth by many hands that have rested there. When I am touched, I creak. Some are afraid to sit in me for fear I might collapse, but some gingerly sit down and rock to and fro. Throb, throb, throb is my pain. Since I am used so little, now I have time to look out the window at a blue sky decked with fleecy clouds, at green grass dotted with yellow dandelions.

Then, reflecting that she might have lived longer if she'd remained a mighty oak, she concluded: *"I do not regret being made into a rocking chair, for I was useful, my arms always wide open to give comfort and pleasure. I watched the children grow, felt their chubby knees as they climbed up on me. 'Whee,' they shrieked, as faster and faster I went back and forth. Then I knew no pain."*

It seemed to me that Verna's fears became less menacing after turning them into original stories. Seeing that she could use her fears as a source of inspiration gave her a sense of accomplishment, and her writing helped her view the challenges of her current situation in the context of her long, rich life.

Deliberately letting our fears loose to transform them into creations gives us a sense of mastery. Try it. Use the topics here to launch your creative writing or make up your own. Compose a song about your fears. Photograph *fear*, finding images to mirror your own. Make up dance movements to represent it. Paint it. Draw a comic strip. Carve or sculpt fears into forms. Make your fears surrealistic if that's how they feel. Depict their enormous power to instruct, if you've seen their beneficial flip side. Exaggerate them. Make fun of them. Fearlessly dip into your experience to extract every drop of color and energy that's there.

Plan to Be Flexible

~

Blessed are the flexible, for they shall not
get bent out of shape.

—ANONYMOUS

My son Timothy and his fiancée, Rachael, have come to visit. Timothy, a professional musician, is on the lanai playing the *didgeridoo*. Its haunting sound sets me down in the Australian outback. Rachael is practicing a lilting classical piece on the piano in the living room.

It's hot. The windows are open. Traffic noises from the highway twenty-one stories below mingle with the music. I sit in my office at my computer. With this book deadline looming, I need to work for a few hours. *Whoa!* Now the didgeridoo sounds like an elephant trumpeting—amazing! I sit here distracted and grateful. Two people I love are close by.

Sounds, even those coming from loved ones, used to make me angry when I was working. I demanded silence, period. When my sons were growing up, I closed my office door and told them not to disturb me unless one of them was bleeding profusely. Now, writing in silence is nice, but it's no longer a requirement.

The ongoing process of learning to be more flexible is not easy. The essence, the heart of flexibility, is seeing whatever presents itself in a given moment and deciding how to respond to it. This is quite different from plowing ahead, responding to what we planned on happening. No wonder this is scary. We're afraid to be flexible because we want solid ground to stand on. We want to know what's next. We want to plan ahead so we can control our agenda, mapping out our day, week, month, or our entire life.

There's only one catch: Often we make up a fine batch of rigid plans only to have them spoiled. Even when we're determined to hang on to our rigidity—usually we call it *organization*—life itself loosens up even the most inflexible of us. The death or illness of one we love, our own accident or sickness, the loss of a job, a natural catastrophe, a violent crime—many unscheduled events get written on our calendars. Our important plans become insignificant when suddenly we must focus on healing a huge heartache, living with ongoing pain, filling out job applications, rebuilding a damaged home, or beginning to heal after being raped. Or maybe our plans don't work out because of all the niggling little things that happen. The car won't start. The babysitter doesn't show up. Our computer crashes.

To face up to how little we really control and how often we need to adapt to new or changing requirements, it helps to change our view of planning. To begin with, we can plan to be flexible, using a pencil with a good eraser. We can learn to congratulate ourselves, not for completing every single item on a "to do" list, but for being fully aware of the ever-changing needs of each moment.

Choose Sanity

The essence of greatness is the ability to choose
personal fulfillment in circumstances where
others choose madness.

—WAYNE DYER

Joan had long, red, exquisitely manicured fingernails. She was midway through her forties, but her smooth hands seemed those of a sixteen-year-old. When I saw her, I felt like tucking my stubby nails and weathered hands into my pockets. But Joan would grab my hand and pull me up close. In a stage whisper, she'd tell one of her many off-color jokes. We'd giggle, and I'd forget about my hands.

Joan lived on the same floor of the nursing home as my stepfather, Andy. When he first moved in, Joan adopted him. She showed him the ropes—introduced him to other residents and filled him in on which staff members to call on and which ones to avoid.

Joan had a degenerative disease that had progressed so far that when I met her she had to be strapped to her wheelchair in order to sit up. Some days she would dig her nails into the palms of her hands and yell for more pain killers. Her husband had left a long time ago, when he found out she was sick. She had no children. She did have a boyfriend, John, a handsome white-haired man in his early fifties. He had suffered a stroke and had a lot of difficulty speaking. Often they sat together in the sun room, holding hands.

Before Joan died, I asked her what kept her going. "My Elvis Presley gospel tapes and prayer," she said.

Joan chose personal fulfillment in circumstances where others might choose madness. There is nothing more poignant than encountering another human being caught in some hell yet bent on creating meaning in the inferno. There is also no fear as great as the one that we ourselves might someday be presented with this challenge. Not one of us wants to crawl down the dark path as Joan had to.

Each of us has a list of awful circumstances we fear might push us over the edge: the death of a child, a prolonged debilitating illness or devastating disability, the loss of all our belongings, rape. Or we wonder how we'd handle it if we made a big mistake that caused irreparable damage to another person or to our own integrity.

If someday you are plunged into a living hell, what could you do? If you're already there, what can you do? Psychiatrist Viktor Frankl endured years in a Nazi death camp and from that experience wrote an invaluable primer for anyone seeking answers to such questions. In *Man's Search for Meaning*, he emphasizes that sanity and the ability to find meaning hinge on making an inner decision not to let outer circumstances destroy the essential part of us.

In extraordinarily fearful situations that threaten your sanity, you can keep that core alive by making one small decision that reflects your unique courage. Then, remembering *I do have a choice*, you can make another decision and another and another.

What might you do? Paint your fingernails red, tell jokes, encourage another, pray, listen to Elvis tapes? When what you choose reflects the wonderful quirkiness of exactly who you are, you can find fulfillment anyplace.

Recon∧truct Your Li∫e

~

Damaged, yes. Broken, no.

—GABRIELE RICO

After you've lost a breast to cancer, a spouse to somebody else, a house to a fire, a job to cutbacks, or any cherished part of your existence, you may feel so splintered that you fear you'll never be whole again. After such losses, it's a common response to awaken predawn, remembering all over again what happened, hearing your mind's convincing dictation, *I just can't go on.*

That message, though as dependable as an alarm clock, is not true. It's a lie we swallow when we're already weakened by fear and drained by anger. Until the moment we die, we can proceed—damaged, but not broken. Even when we're missing elements of life we'd imagined were absolutely essential, we can, in time, reconstruct our life, even if it's without those precious parts.

Reconstruction becomes possible when we allow ourselves to experience the five-step grieving process that Elisabeth Kübler-Ross identified. Its stages are: denial and isolation, anger, bargaining, depression, and, finally, acceptance. In this process, we zigzag back and forth, visiting and revisiting the initial stages, until finally we get an inkling, often just a grudging acknowledgment, that it's possible we might find some acceptance of our altered situation. At this point, the question we pose to ourselves is as tentative as a kid about to ride his or her bicycle minus the training wheels for the first time: *Do you suppose I can?*

As we move into acceptance, we don't feel brave, but we are. Our courage is not a constant smile or a cheerful Pollyanna voice. It is not testifying to ourselves or anybody else how lucky we are to be so harshly tested by life.

Often acceptance is not animated or enthusiastic—it simply is. We're still unhappy about what's happened. We still despise the ill fate that led us into this situation. But when we begin to embrace acceptance, we're doing it out of sheer desperation simply because it's dawning on us that it's the only flight available that will lift us out of despair.

Acceptance is a shift in focus and perspective that transforms fear, changing half-empty lives into half-full ones. In acceptance, each day we decide over and over again that we'll stop sucking empty air into our straws; instead, we aim deep into the core of ourselves, drawing in the nourishing liquid fullness that remains. In making this choice, we begin to appreciate what we have left.

Recently, I read about Sudha Chandran, a contemporary classical dancer from India who had to have her left leg amputated. After she was fitted with an artificial leg, she began to perform again. When asked how, she answered, "You don't need feet to dance."

There is a deep joy we earn in going on, as Sudha has, in refusing to be broken—in wandering through the maze of fear and not giving up until we find the opening that leads to acceptance. Bravo to Sudha Chandran. Bravo to you and me and to millions of men and women, past, present, and future, who sustain damage but ultimately refuse to be broken.

Laugh About Uncertainty

If we had the luxury of certainty,

we wouldn't need courage.

—ROBERT J. FUREY, PH.D.

Not long ago, at an international conference, the Dalai Lama was asked, "What do you think is going to happen in the world fifty years from now?" Others had already stated their predictions, but his response, accompanied by a deep belly laugh, was simply, "Madam, I don't know what kind of tea I'll be having for dinner tonight. How am I supposed to know what's going to happen in the world fifty years from now?"

This wise and gentle man was not always so at ease with uncertainty. In fact, many years before, when he was only nineteen years old, he sat down with Communist Chinese leaders and calmly outlined his reasons why Tibetan Buddhists should be allowed to return to their country to practice Buddhism without restrictions or recriminations. He felt sure the high-ranking officials would listen to his obviously sound logic. As the world knows, they did not. At this writing, he and thousands of Tibetans remain in exile, and Chinese oppression of those who have remained in Tibet continues.

Gaining enough serenity to laugh about uncertainty is the result of first awakening to the reality that certainty is impossible and then resolving to do the best we can minus that luxury. When you feel your courage evaporating in the face of uncertainty, ask yourself, *What do I wish I knew for certain?* Jot down or say aloud all the big and little things—anything that occurs to you. For instance: "I wish I knew if my car is going to last another six months without a major repair bill." "I wish I knew if I was going to pass the bar exam." "I wish I could be

sure that the baby I'm expecting will be healthy and normal."
"I wish I could be sure my wife won't start using cocaine again."

Now look at your list and ask yourself, *Is there anything I can do to up the odds that the outcome I desire will happen?* As in these examples, might you get a tune-up and an oil change, study more, have regular prenatal exams, or accept that you can only love a mate, not give her the strength to kick an addiction?

Once we clarify what our efforts need to be, we can focus on them. And then having tried our best, we can sigh in relief. Many outcomes are simply beyond our control. Our one and only responsibility is to know what we value and to devote energy to these priorities.

Life for all of us is uncertain. Our courage grows, despite uncertainty, when we know one thing—that "for sure" we're attending to the business of daily living.

Comfort Others Who Are Just as Scared as You Are

~

Raise your right hand against fear.
Extend the other in compassion.

—SHELDON KOPP

T he two sentences above are the title and subtitle of Sheldon Kopp's insightful book about confronting and managing fear, a subject with which the author is intimately acquainted. Twenty-five years ago, he found out he had a brain tumor. Since then, he's had to face ongoing pain, being partially crippled, and the probability of progressively debilitating handicaps. He's also given readers a number of books that are full of compassion about the human condition, and he and his wife have raised three sons.

Kopp's life and work are reminders that we don't have to wait until we're fearless to become compassionate human beings. Even while we're shaking with fear, we can shake another person's hand. Even though we feel paralyzed with fright, we can pick up the phone and speak to someone else who needs comforting. By consoling one another, we actually set into motion our own healing.

Of necessity, it takes a while to realize this. When we're scared, we tend to become extremely self-centered. We sense that to survive we'll have to face our fear and find ways to manage it. We know that out-of-control fear could rip us apart. Concern for others is not a high priority when we're busy attempting to save our own skin.

But we don't have to stay focused exclusively on ourselves. We don't have to become masters at fighting our own fear before we begin to help others extinguish theirs. By facing our fears, we put ourselves on the path of courage. By extending a hand to others who are struggling, we receive extra energy to walk further down that path.

It takes considerable effort to break out of our isolation and to actually do this. Logic may tell us we have nothing worthwhile to give just yet. But we do. I am always amazed at whatever grace it is that descends on us, allowing and assisting one frightened human being to enter into a compassionate exchange with another. It simply happens when we go ahead and try.

A few days ago, two friends and I visited a dying neighbor in the hospital. I had hesitated to come along. What could I say to her, when I was in the midst of confronting some heavy, ongoing fears of my own? I couldn't find many words, so I held her hand. Barely conscious, she spoke up clearly, "Your hand's so cool; it feels so good on my warm skin." The iciness in my hand was actually the chill of fear. But my coolness lifted her spirits. And her warmth, her words, gave me courage.

Sheldon Kopp likens our human journey to walking the refugee road. He reminds us that what really matters is that *"we care for any other frightened children we might meet along the way!"*

Savor Your Beautiful Moments

The unendurable is the beginning of the curve of joy.

—DJUNA BARNES

I t's not culturally acceptable to be afraid for very long. Though it's okay to experience *moments* of fear, we're expected to move on quickly out of their shadows into sunny optimism. But the fears that often come along with illness, new adventures, or loss often won't budge for days or even months. Some of them may, in fact, never disappear entirely, and unless we face them and endure them, they will not dissipate or be transformed. Though we may not receive a lot of validation, remaining present to fears that seem unendurable is a heroic task with great rewards.

Carol is a teacher in her late forties. One morning four months ago, she found out she had breast cancer. The next day, she had a lumpectomy, followed by radiation treatments. Since then, fear has been her daily companion. At times it's overwhelmingly huge; other times it's napping in the backseat. But it never leaves entirely. Sometimes her whole body starts shaking. An ache or pain makes her wonder if cancer is staking a new claim somewhere. Immersing herself in work always helped in the past, but it doesn't help now. She used to love to travel, but since her surgery, being away from home only magnifies her fears. "Unfortunately, I have to take myself along," she says, "and I'm not very good company right now."

Carol's always been strong and competent, the person everyone admires and leans on. She's run marathons and volunteers at a hospice. She's a loving wife and mother and a listening ear for family and friends. Now no one can understand why she can't walk straight away from her fears. Uneasy with her raw terror, those close to her are encouraging her to get on with life.

Carol's as uneasy as those who love her. She always took good health, abundant stamina, and a long life for granted. But her new fears have shaken her to the core, forcing her to take an extended tour "through the valley of the shadow of death," which David referred to in Psalm 23.

Carol is, however, surprised and grateful for this unexpected outcome. Even in this descent into terror, she's beginning to find moments of pure joy. Making love with her husband of twenty years feels brand-new, almost unbearably intense and tender. When she pours a cup of tea, she refuses to hurry, inhaling the aroma and savoring each sip. Standing in line at the bank has turned into an opportunity for meditation, not aggravation. Her teenager's marathon phone conversations don't bother her much anymore. And knowing, truly knowing now that we're all transients on this earth, she feels a heightened compassion for herself and others. She laughs more and judges less.

No one likes to be confronted with a situation that stirs up terrible, ongoing fears, but there are priceless lessons that we can learn while enduring them. Most can't be absorbed instantly. We have to hit bottom, muck around down there for a while, and eventually do a ragged zigzag dance up into joy. Like it or not, we're permanently shaken but also forever wiser.

Don't Allow Fear to Take Up Too Much Space

⁓

When any experience of body, heart, or mind keeps
repeating in consciousness, it is a signal that this visi-
tor is asking for a deeper and fuller attention.

—JACK KORNFIELD

There are times when we've done everything we can think of to cope with an ongoing fear. We've identified it. We've felt it over and over. But our attention isn't helping. Instead of becoming easier to handle, it's getting worse. For instance: "I'm afraid of the Friday planning sessions my boss began scheduling. She's eager for my input, but I liked it better when she just *assigned* tasks to me. I'm terrified about voicing my opinions, and she's forcing me to make major decisions. I thought I'd get over this, but I dread that hour more and more. It's making me a nervous wreck."

To uncover what keeps reigniting persistent fears such as this, one may need deeper scrutiny. Therapy, regular meditation, or gentle self-examination may help us discover several underlying reasons for our fear. Meanwhile, as we unravel its complex causes, we may also need immediate relief to keep it from completely enveloping us and permeating every cell in our body. Otherwise, instead of I HAVE *this fear,* it starts to feel as if I AM *this fear.*

Though you may not be able to launch your fear into outer space, you can keep it from freely roaming all over you by making a special place for it in one part of your body. First, set aside a time simply to observe your fear. No doubt you *think* about it a lot, but for now, clear your mind of speculation about it. Just pay close attention to the physical sensations it stirs up and note the form it's taking. Is it a gray fog, so cold you can't stop shivering? A thick starch poured over your entire body, making it so stiff you can hardly move? A hard rock in your throat that's keeping you from breathing? A sad colorless ache that makes your heart feel heavy? A turbulent churning in your solar plexus?

Once you've observed it closely and experienced its sensations, close your eyes and relax. Now imagine exactly what kind of housing accommodations you want to give your fear and where in your body you want it to stay.

Jed, a shy young man who'd moved a thousand miles away from family and friends and was increasingly afraid of making new friends, describes what happened when he tried this: "My fear was a thousand butterflies in my stomach. Some of them flew up into my throat, others down into my knees. They made me nauseated, took my voice away, and turned my knees into Jell-O. I decided they deserved no more than a tiny wire cage in the right side of my belly."

The next time Jed met someone he wanted to get to know better, he took a deep breath and visualized the butterflies confined to their small cage. "Each time they tried to escape, I kept them there. For the first time in months, my fear was small enough that I actually enjoyed a conversation."

Our fear can take over so completely that we begin to believe it's us. But it's not. An entrepreneur who has to keep subduing her fear of becoming a bag lady puts it like this: "We have to tell our fear repeatedly, in no uncertain terms: *You can have a small piece of me but not all.*"

Hug This Moment

~

Only death is no trouble.

—JOSEPH CAMPBELL

Do you fear that life will never settle down into a comfortable, rewarding routine? Are you afraid the day will never come when you have it all together? Tragedies, pain, losses, as well as aggravations and inconveniences are present in all our lives in varying degrees. Some of life's troubles move in as permanent residents, and we are given the opportunity to learn from them for the rest of our lives. Others stay long enough to teach us briefer, but crucial, lessons. Even our joys bring along responsibilities—think of babies, gardens, even vacations.

Four years ago, a dear friend of mine, Bryan, died at age forty-one. Bryan ran a large construction company, loved his wife and two teenaged children, was an active volunteer in his church, and skied his beloved Colorado's slopes as often as he could. The evening he suffered a fatal aneurysm, he'd spent an exhilarating day in Breckenridge, skiing with his family.

Of all the people I've known well who have passed from this life, Bryan exuded the most intense attitude of taking life as it came, troubles and all, and of partaking of each day fully. He was never caught up. His life had loose ends that sprouted like dandelions everywhere, and he'd gone through sadness, disillusionment, and disappointment. But Bryan manifested on a daily basis the philosophy that life, even with all its troubles, is worth living.

Viewing Bryan's body, I felt an overwhelming sadness. The animation in his face, his expression that indicated he was ready for all earth's joys and trials, was gone, leaving a totally peaceful mask—not Bryan.

Not long ago, I found out that Joseph Campbell, the anthropologist and author who wrote the quote that begins this essay, is buried right across the street from my Honolulu apartment. There is a sense of serenity in the beautiful old cemetery. I like to sit on a stone bench that faces the bronze plaque marking Campbell's grave. Usually mynah birds are chirping close by. Often a pineapple shower, Hawaii's amazingly gentle, warm spray of raindrops, tickles my arms.

Last time I was there, I reflected on my current harder-than-usual struggle to embrace all of my troubles and thought about Bryan and Joseph Campbell. I wished I could ask them, "How did you so fully grasp that life, even when it's irritating or awful, is a precious privilege?" I imagine that their answers would point me back to the wisdom that is already within you and me: *Only death is no trouble.* The reality is that our ability to breathe is all we ultimately need to turn loose and enjoy life "as is."

Right now, take the time to embrace your life without the nagging fear that it won't get better. Hug this moment, not the one ahead that you hope will be different. Encircle it with a warm thank you, even if tears are in your eyes and despair is in your heart. Make this simple expression of your gratitude often each day, silently or out loud. It is the one sure way that life is guaranteed to be better no matter what your circumstances.

Be Brave Enough
to Accept Wisdom

People are afraid to become wise.

—LYNN ANDREWS

F acing and feeling our fears is a habit all us can acquire and practice for the rest of our lives. You already know how: Each time fear arises, dare to be with it. Admit its reality. Feel its presence. Remain open to understanding its cause.

The process is certainly simple enough, but there's one formidable catch: It's far from easy, because consistently submitting to this straightforward way of handling fear leads to wisdom. And while *being* wise is a desirable state, *becoming* wise can be difficult and frightening for a variety of reasons.

For one thing, there's no time off for good behavior. Just because we faced a really big fear yesterday, there's no guarantee that another huge one won't need attention today. Besides, gigantic fears, showing no mercy or consideration, often arrive when we're already booked solid with an aggravating assortment of lesser ones. And so on the day you lose your job, your cat disappears, you find out your mother is dying, and the washing machine won't spin. Consciously facing and feeling so many fears may seem like too much, so we're tempted to go back to trying to run from them.

The responsibilities that come with facing and feeling our fears can be terrifying too. So long as our fears keep mushrooming into demons and monsters, we have little choice but to focus on survival. But once we've begun to calm our fears, the spotlight can move off of us. And when it does, we have a chance to look around and see the fears and needs of others. After a few months, or maybe it will take a few years, our hearts will warm with compassion not only for our own predicaments but also for those of friends and neighbors, for those we once perceived as "enemies," and for the entire planet. And we'll feel accountable for finding ways to be kind to ourselves and others.

No doubt many of you have already discovered these and other perils, and you're doubting that you're up to accepting the wisdom that comes with facing and feeling your fears. We encourage you not to get permanently stuck in despair. Finding excuses, feeling uncertain, and clinging to the status quo are all natural and infinitely human, last-ditch attempts to sidestep wisdom. Few of us are convinced that we're ready to handle the demands that wisdom makes on us. We're all scared silly of becoming wise.

What can help us over this enormous hump is making a commitment to face only one fear at a time—first this one, then the next one, and then the next. When we do this, one by one, each tough confrontation goes into a pile with the others until, in an amazing alchemy, our humble efforts become transformed into courage.

As this hard-won courage grows inside us, slowly we begin to accept wisdom, to comprehend its value, and to decipher its map. In wisdom, there are many pathways to growing awareness, to deeper serenity, to sturdier acceptance, to unconditional, irrevocable joy and peace. Every single frightened effort we make to keep on crawling out from under the covers takes us a little deeper into wisdom's treasure-strewn territory.

Invite Courage in
Again and Again

~

Courage is resistance to fear, mastery of
fear—not absence of fear.

—MARK TWAIN

H ere are nine reminders to help you keep summoning courage anytime you need it. They are principles you know but can easily lose sight of when you're afraid:

1. *You will feel fear.* You may hate it and wish you could escape from it, but you will experience it in varying degrees at different times throughout your life.

2. *Courage grows the moment you face your fear.* Resist *thinking* about fear—*experience* it. The first step, the hardest one, is to acknowledge fear, to see it, and to look it directly in the eye.

3. *Courage is already inside you.* Trust yourself and let courage lead you where you must go or show you what you have to do. When necessary, sit and wait for a while until its truth can be deciphered.

4. *Your fear can teach you lessons as you face it.* You may think its lessons are cruel, unnecessary, or dumb, but they all will serve as teachers so long as you remain open to learning. You will understand more about these messages as time goes by.

5. *Listen to fear's message, then feel free to disagree.* Fear may be telling you to stop, proceed with caution, or run as fast as you can. There are times to comply and times to push past fear, telling it to get lost.

6. *Clarity increases with ongoing practice.* Each time you face a fear and feel it, the more you will understand it and

all your other fears. When you know fear's nature better, you see you have a choice—you can manage fear rather than let it manage you. It does not have to dictate your actions or dominate your life.

7. *Fears that are ignored, denied, criticized, condemned, repressed, or minimized will grow.* Just notice all your fears. Accept them. Admit they exist without putting yourself down, sweeping them under the rug, or saying they really don't bother you.

8. *Sometimes, even though you're aware of all this, you'll be too tired, or you'll be caught off guard, or you'll forget you know.* When this happens, you'll be overcome by fear, and you'll wonder if you can ever again find your lost courage.

9. *When you regress, remember: There is still a seed of courage within you, and you can choose to cultivate it.* Courageous people are persistent, not perfect. With great compassion for yourself, try again. Resolve to make friends with your fears by facing them and feeling them one more time. You can transform your fears simply by being aware of them again and again.

Other Helpful Reading

You must understand the whole of life, not just one
little part of it. That is why you must read, that is why
you must look at the skies, that is why you must sing,
and dance, and write poems, and suffer, and
understand, for all that is life.

—J. KRISHNAMURTI

These authors are a colorful, mismatched bunch, not at all alike in their approaches. What they do have in common is that each explores facing, feeling, and transforming fear with great insight. The books that follow were like a wise circle of brave and honest friends surrounding Marilyn and me while we were writing. Sometimes we disagreed with their conclusions; other times they affirmed our hunches and validated our experiences. Often they stretched our thinking, leading us to discard not-so-useful ideas, try on more serviceable ones, and weave entirely new ones. May you find the right ones to keep you company, to nourish your soul, and to deepen your understanding.

Arkoff, Abe. *The Illuminated Life.* Boston: Allyn and Bacon, 1995.

Arkoff, a clinical psychologist and professor emeritus of psychology at the University of Hawaii, invites readers to "illuminate" their lives by systematic self-examination. I have never run across a more comprehensive approach to self-awareness. To facilitate the process, each of the fourteen chapters asks one pointed question. Of particular help as we face our fears is the chapter "Coping: How Do I Manage

Stress, Threat, and Challenge?" Officially, this is a college textbook, so it costs a little extra. But in my opinion, its 498 readable, courage-inspiring pages are well worth it.

Bourne, Edmund J., Ph.D. *The Anxiety and Phobia Workbook.* Oakland, Calif.: New Harbinger, 1990.

This step-by-step guide for moving out of an overwhelming level of anxiety and panic covers everything from relaxation, desensitization, and changing beliefs to nutrition and medication. An excellent daily reference to help you lessen anxiety and either manage or overcome a phobia.

Chödrön, Pema. *The Wisdom of No Escape and the Path of Loving-Kindness.* Boston & London: Shambhala, 1991.

_____. *When Thing Fall Apart: Heart Advice for Difficult Times.* Boston & London: Shambhala, 1996.

_____. *The Places That Scare You: A Guide to Fearlessness in Difficult Times.* Boston & London: Shambhala, 2001.

If you're fearing that your life will never get any better, and you may not either, read these books by an American Buddhist nun. She gently reminds us to befriend ourselves *just as we are* and to be satisfied with what we already have. Meditation is the framework for her wise teaching, but her counsel should be encouraging to anybody who is longing to find contentment. My own copy of *When Things Fall Apart* has literally fallen apart I've consulted it so often. In it, Chödrön insists that feelings like "disappointments, embarrassment, irritation, resentment, anger, jealousy, and fear, instead of being bad news, are actually very clear moments that teach us where it is that we're holding back.... They're like messenagers that show us, with terrifying clarity, exactly where we're stuck." All three books are wise primers about remaining spiritual warriors in the midst of fluctuating emotions and changing circumstances.

Cookson, Catherine. *Let Me Make Myself Plain.* London: Transworld, 1989.

In these essays and poems, the popular English novelist lets readers in on many struggles from her long life, including living with chronic illnesses and recovering from a nervous breakdown. She's indomitable, feisty, vulnerable, frail, and ultimately courageous. She knows from experience that we can stop being kicked around by the thoughts that "accompany depression, and worry, and sick anxiety." I keep rereading parts of this one—her eloquent honesty made me think, if she can keep on subduing her fears, I can too.

Davis, Martha, Ph.D., Elizabeth Robbins Eshelman, M.S.W., and Matthew McKay, Ph.D. *The Relaxation and Stress Reduction Workbook.* Oakland, Calif.: New Harbinger, 1980 (Fourth Edition, revised in 1995).

Overly stressed people are very afraid they simply cannot handle circumstances they perceive of as "dangerous, difficult, or painful." Here the authors invite readers to change their appraisals of what's happening and to master skills that build confidence in coping. This intelligent, comprehensive workbook gives very clear directions on a variety of tools we can learn to use, including progressive relaxation, nutrition, thought stopping, and assertiveness training.

Frankl, Viktor E. *Man's Search for Meaning.* New York: Simon & Schuster, 1984 (originally published in Austria in 1946).

Frankl, an internationally renowned psychiatrist, writes a graphic account of his experiences in a Nazi death camp during World War II. Out of the living hell, Frankl sculpted a new approach to psychotherapy known as *logotherapy,* which he also outlines here. At its core is Frankl's belief in "the human capacity to creatively turn life's negative aspects into something positive or constructive." We can, he asserts, say "yes to life in spite of everything." There is tremendous honesty, astounding courage, and ultimately great hope in these pages. I highly recommend this perceptive guide; I keep it within easy reach.

Furey, Robert J., Ph.D. *Facing Fear: The Search for Courage.* New York: Alba House, 1990.

Furey, a psychotherapist, writes, "When we reach those points in our lives where we really need courage, seldom are we looking for intricate, mysterious philosophies." With this in mind, he has written simply, deeply, and concisely about this quest. In only 114 pages, he draws on his own ideas and intersperses stories and quotes from Dr. Seuss, John F. Kennedy, Abraham Maslow, and many others. Of particular interest to those who can't seem to shake a fear of disapproval is a chapter called "Dealing with the Fear of People." Other chapters include confronting the fear of life, daring to dream, choosing to act, and pursuing one's special calling. For young adults trying to find the courage to be themselves, there are many sturdy suggestions. For older readers who know all too well that the quest never ends, there's plenty of encouragement too.

Harrison, Gavin. *In the Lap of the Buddha.* Boston & London: Shambhala, 1994.

Harrison, a teacher of insight meditation, was diagnosed HIV positive in 1989. In a deeply moving spiritual exploration, he offers insights into how we can use the suffering such life-threatening crises inflict on us to grow wiser and more compassionate. One chapter, "Beyond the Grip of Fear," is particularly powerful as he reminds readers that "patience is vital when grappling with fear" and encourages us to remember that "a place of fear may well be a place of great potential and understanding."

Jeffers, Susan, Ph.D. *Feel the Fear and Do It Anyway.* New York: Ballantine, 1987.

Whether you are facing the fears built into loss or grief or are scared to take a risk or embark on an adventure, Jeffers suggests ways to strengthen your spirituality while taking concrete steps toward conquering fear. For instance, if you're afraid of making decisions, she includes a reassuring chapter, "How to Make a No-Lose Decision," and outlines exactly how to go about doing this. This is an exceptionally insightful and practical book, one to keep rereading and consulting.

Kopp, Sheldon. *Raise Your Right Hand Against Fear, Extend the Other in Compassion.* New York: Ballantine, 1990.

Continuing to face our fears not only makes our own journey easier, but it also gives us compassion for others who are just as frightened as we are. Kopp, an eminent psychologist and author, makes this his central theme in these 150 pages. Kopp's books are never typical "self-help" volumes. Here he tells spellbinding stories of the evolution of his own fears with a frankness and eloquence usually reserved for fiction. Throughout, he interjects practical, wise counsel on dealing with fear, not shying away from such difficult topics as looking at what we fear most within ourselves, experiencing terror when there's no real threat, becoming so scared that we hide who we really are, and deciding when to take bold action and when to exercise caution. Whereas some authors seem too afraid—or are simply unable to delve deeply into the topic of fear—Kopp is not. His fearlessness inspires me to do the hard work of fearlessness—to keep on facing my fears. This is a "must read."

Kornfield, Jack. *A Path with Heart: A Guide Through the Perils and Promises of Spiritual Life.* New York: Bantam, 1993.

Kornfield, a renowned teacher, psychologist, and meditation master, emphasizes that there are many spiritual practices—many paths with heart—but he focuses here on the one he's taken: meditation rooted in Buddhism. In meditation, he emphasizes, we don't find endless transcendent bliss. Rather, we have opportunities to face all our thoughts and feelings as they arise. "When we let ourselves feel the fear, the discontent, the difficulties we have always avoided, our heart softens," he writes. This guide is especially valuable because Kornfield shows, by his own example and with many stories, how our spirituality can bloom and deepen, how we can become more fearless in the midst of it all—as we're rocking the baby, fixing dinner, or even preparing to die. Whether you're thinking of beginning to practice meditation or have been meditating for years, I highly recommend this wise and balanced guide.

Krishnamurti, J. *The First & Last Freedom.* San Francisco: HarperCollins, 1975 (originally published in 1954).

This eminent spiritual teacher often talked and wrote about fear. Here he discusses fear, sex, gossip, suffering, awareness, self-deception, and many more topics. Of fear, he writes, "Fear comes into being when I desire to be in a particular pattern. When I demand a particular way of living that in itself is a source of fear. My difficulty is my desire to live in a certain frame. Can I not break the frame?" If you have a philosophical bent, most likely you'll find Krishnamurti's discourses intriguing and valuable.

Markova, Dawna, Ph.D. *No Enemies Within.* Berkeley: Conari Press, 1994.

This is an excellent resource to help us develop courage to meet the fears within ourselves. Markova, who many years ago was cured of "terminal" cancer, is currently a consultant to individuals and groups about the uses of creativity for change. "Healing," she writes, "insists that you reexamine everything—all of your habits, ideas, beliefs, values, passions, inhibitions, assumptions—until you find those things that are truest at the core, discarding everything else." To assist us, Markova gently and expertly hands readers a treasury of profound yet simple insights and exercises.

Reynolds, David K. *Constructive Living.* Honolulu: University of Hawaii Press, 1984.

A couple of years ago when I had the energy level of a slug for one long and very frightening year, this little green book inspired me to do the small "somethings" I could, preventing me from permanently becoming one with my living room couch. The essence of *constructive living,* which is based on Morita Therapy, is to live constructively no matter how you're feeling at the moment. Morita, a Japanese psychiatrist, was a contemporary of Freud. Reynolds, a therapist and the leading Western authority on Japanese psychotherapies, writes, "The mature human being goes about doing what needs to be done regardless of whether that person feels great or terrible." Reynolds is not advocating ignoring feelings. If you're afraid, acknowledge your fear and feel it, he advises. But then he reminds us to ask ourselves, What do I need to be doing now? And, of course, he presses on to urge us to do the hard part—to go ahead and do it. If you're having a tough time, read this.

Thich Nhat Hanh. *The Miracle of Mindfulness: A Manual in Meditation.* Boston: Beacon Press, 1975.

In this exceptionally clear and practical guide to meditation, Vietnamese Zen master Thich Nhat Hanh gently reminds readers of "the essential discipline of following one's breath to nourish and maintain calm mindfulness even in the midst of the most difficult circumstances." These basic instructions are appropriate not only for Buddhists but also for those of all beliefs. Because he believes that the mindful state of meditation should spill over into more awareness in all that we do, he includes simple exercises to teach us exactly how, including for when we wake up in the morning, wash dishes, or carry on a conversation. The wide-awake living he proposes runs counter to our anesthetized Western culture and offers a powerful alternative—to be "present" to everything, including our big and little fears.

_____. *Peace Is Every Step: The Path of Mindfulness in Everyday Life.* New York: Bantam, 1991.

It's hard to read only one book by Thich Nhat Hanh. This more recent one, assembled from his lectures, published and unpublished writings, and informal conversations, is full of more of his deep simple teachings, including five steps to transform fear. As his editor writes in an introduction, the essence of Thich Nhat Hanh's message is "that peace is not external or to be sought after or attained. Living mindfully, slowing down, and enjoying each step and each breath, is enough." Just seeing those words on my computer screen calms my fears, right now.

Trungpa, Chögyam. *Shambhala: The Sacred Path of the Warrior.* Boston & London: Shambhala, 1984.

Are you a "warrior," dedicating yourself to finding courage and living a life of compassion and meaning, or are you slouching down into cowardice, avoiding challenges, running scared? Here, Trungpa, a Tibetan Buddhist meditation master and teacher, outlines explicitly what staying on the warrior's sacred path entails, including a chapter called "Fear and Fearlessness." This is a very wise guide to practicing courage.

Valles, Carlos G. *Let Go of Fear.* New York: Triumph, 1991.

"It is to our own advantage to give ourselves the freedom to look at our own fears without shame or misgivings, rather than artificially pretend we are not afraid of anything. We *are* afraid, and we should be the first to know it and own up to it," writes Valles, author of many books and a Spanish Jesuit who has worked in India for forty years. With that premise as a foundation, Valles's essays look at fear from many different angles. In "Let the Worst Happen," for example, he challenges readers to get to the point where they can finally say, "So what?" Another powerful essay examines how faith in Jesus leads to defeating fear. Valles's illustrations flow out of the culture of India and are fresh and enlightening.

Wallis, Velma. *Two Old Women: An Alaska Legend of Betrayal, Courage and Survival.* New York: Harper-Collins, 1994.

This short book, based on an Athabascan Indian legend, is one to read anytime you're afraid you can't go on. It's a powerful tale, well told, of what happens to two old women abandoned by their tribe during a brutal winter famine. They find inner resources, stamina, and survival skills they never dreamed they could resurrect. Even with plenty of aches and pains, even with frequent fear and sporadic depression, even with great sadness over being left to die, they persevere. The story is, as a review in *Kirkus* notes, "an octogenarian version of 'Thelma and Louise' triumphant."

Zukav, Gary. *The Seat of the Soul.* New York: Simon & Schuster, 1990 (first published in 1989).

Zukav contends that the pursuit of external power such as more money and more status is ultimately destructive, whereas "power that is based upon the perceptions and values of the spirit" enriches the world and gives life meaning and purpose. Because much of our fear is based either on losing something we have or not getting something we want, Zukav's philosophy, if we can actually learn to take stock in it, is bound to reduce the level of our fears. When I was the most terrified about living with permanent neurological impairments, I clung to passages such as: "Within each experience of pain or negativity is the opportunity to challenge the perception that lies behind it, the fear that lies behind it, and to choose to learn with wisdom. The fear will not vanish immediately, but it will disintegrate as you work with courage. When fear ceases to scare you, it cannot stay." If soul food like this is what you're hungry for, you'll find it in abundance here.

Acknowledgments

Marilyn's and Sarah's Acknowledgments

We need to honor your anonymity, but we want every single one of you whom we interviewed about facing fear and finding courage to know how much your stories and observations inspired us. We regret not having enough space to include all your contributions. Your spirits, your courageousness breathe life into every page.

We nominate Mary Jane Ryan as "Best Editor." We don't understand how she does it—she extends complete trust to us and makes a shelter for our originality while also interjecting her keen discernment. Then, finally, she marks up the manuscript with such perception and precision that we end up saying much more exactly what we'd meant to say in the first place. Once again, this second time around, we thank you.

Sarah's Acknowledgments

Initially, my son Timothy was part of our writing team. Though he decided not to continue, he helped shape the book's concepts and focus, urging that it should speak more to the heart than to the intellect, reminding, "You need to *feel* fear, not *think* about it." He read many essays and made specific suggestions for rewriting—ferreting out clichés, homing in on erroneous assumptions, and contributing fresh images and ideas. Thanks, Timothy, for all your valuable contributions.

My son Matthew read the many quotations under consideration for inclusion in the book and responded to them by adding his own comments. "The cause of fear, for me, boils down to a lack of certainty in what the future holds," he concluded. Now in his late twenties, he speaks, I believe, for the majority of young men and women. Thanks, Matt. I value your honest and astute perceptions. I also appreciate your ongoing affirmation and encouragement.

My husband, Jack, did more than his share at home, bringing home groceries, cooking, or suggesting, "Why don't we go out for dinner." He kept encouraging me even when I was at my computer so long that I skipped many of our mutual activities. Thank you for loving me "as is," for offering wise feedback, for providing technical information, and for continuing to inspire me with your courage and optimism.

I thank you, Mother, for the precious gift of life, for all your caregiving, and for talking honestly with me about some of the fearful parts of your long journey.

My friends LuAnn Budzianowski, Naomi Gaede-Penner, and Christine Morita kept sending me excellent resource material and quotes on fear. They also made astute suggestions for changes. Christine went over the manuscript thoroughly, finding grammatical goofs, typos, and adding refreshing ideas. Thank you all for your contributions and encouragement.

The "regulars" at the Monday night Facing Fear, Finding Courage support group traveled with me through an extended "dark night of the soul." You all know how close I came to giving up. God bless you for holding me up in prayer, with hugs, and by sharing your own journeys. Thanks to Gus Callbeck, David Cox, Mapu Gusman, Kay McMahon, and Ed Steele. And Liz Ishikawa—I hold your smile and your courage in loving memories.

The Illuminated Life study group offered loving support. Thank you Abe Arkoff for writing our amazing textbook. I appreciate encouragement and shared insights from you and from Liz Bailey, Josita Calhoun, and Dorothy Harrison, fellow souls who've become dear friends.

Other gifted encouragers have my deepest gratitude: Christine and Gary Gurley, Jetta and Larry Feil, Margaret Hadley, Bill and Lydia Hilliard, Kathy Lau, Connie Ning, Sarah Oktay, Ellie Rogers, Nina and Jerry Spotts, Rachael Timberlake, Cathy Yeargan, and Judy White.

Blessings to these accomplished helpers and healers: Maryann Gianantoni, Patti Herrera, Dr. Ira Keisman, Dr. Kenneth Nakano, David Nakashima, and Yoshio Saruwatari.

Marilyn's Acknowledgments

My wonderful friends have constantly been a source of inspiration and encouragement: Lyle Johnson, Bruce Kaye, Angela Grandinelli, Chris Bonner, Archie Evans, Glenn Niebling, and Pat Boots. Thanks for your continued devotion and loyalty throughout this writing project.

Index